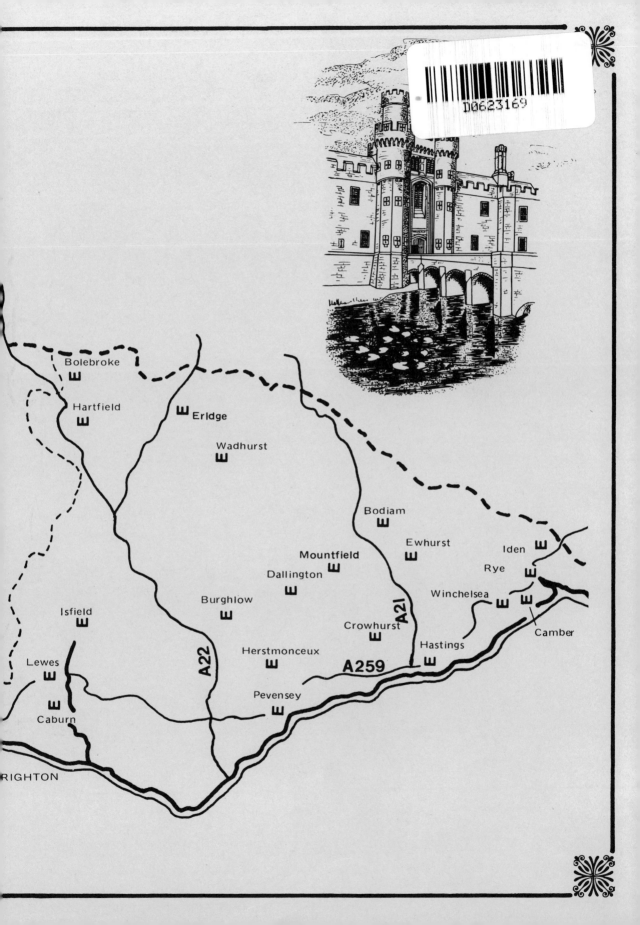

Bolebroke

Hartfield

Eridge

Wadhurst

Bodiam

Ewhurst

Iden

Mountfield

Dallington

Rye

Winchelsea

Burghlow

Isfield

Crowhurst

Camber

Hastings

A21

Lewes

Herstmonceux

A22

A259

Caburn

Pevensey

RIGHTON

CASTLES IN SUSSEX

CASTLES
in
SUSSEX

John Guy

Phillimore

1984

Published by
PHILLIMORE & CO. LTD.
Shopwyke Hall, Chichester, Sussex

ISBN 0 85033 523 X

Printed and bound in Great Britain by
THE CAMELOT PRESS LTD
Southampton, England

I dedicate this book
to the best and dearest friend
I ever had

'This royal throne of Kings, this scepter'd isle,
This earth of majesty, this seat of Mars,
This other Eden, demi-paradise,
This fortress built by Nature for herself
Against infection and the hand of war,
This happy breed of men, this little world,
This precious stone set in the silver sea,
Which serves it in the office of a wall,
Or as a moat defensive to a house,
Against the envy of less happier lands;
This blèssed plot, this earth, this realm, this England . . .'

William Shakespeare
John of Gaunt in *Richard II*

CONTENTS

List of illustrations   ix
List of plans   xi
Acknowledgements   xiii

Introduction   1

Castles in Sussex   11
Amberley, Arundel, Bodiam, Bramber, Camber, Chichester, Cowdray, Crowhurst, Hastings, Herstmonceux, Knepp Old Castle, Lewes, Petworth House, Pevensey, Rye, Winchelsea

Lost and Minor Castles   123
Aldingbourne, Burghlow, Caburn, Earnley, Ewhurst, Fulking, Hartfield, Iden, Midhurst, Old Erringham, Pulborough, Rogate, Rudgwick, Sedgwick, Shoreham, Verdley

Later and Sham Castles   137
Bolebroke, Castle Goring, Coates, Dallington Old Castle, Eridge, Isfield Place, Knepp New Castle, Wadhurst

LIST OF ILLUSTRATIONS

Page

1. Aerial view of Selham Castle 2
2. Aerial view of Bramber Castle 3
3. Aerial view of Knepp Old Castle 4
4. Aerial view of Arundel Castle 4
5. Camber Castle viewed from the north-west 8
6. Eridge Castle, a 19th-century lithograph 9
7. Entrance front, Castle Goring 10
8. Aerial view of Amberley Castle 12
9. Gatehouse of Amberley Castle, a 19th-century print .. 14
10. The garderobe tower, Amberley Castle 15
11. West front, Amberley Castle 16
12. The north front, Amberley Castle 18
13. Arundel Castle's 19th-century reconstruction work 20
14. The upper ward, Arundel Castle 23
15. The shell keep, Arundel Castle 23
16. Outer gatehouse and barbican, Arundel Castle 25
17. Reconstructed state apartments, Arundel Castle 27
18. The barbican towers, Arundel Castle 28
19. The entrance front, Bodiam Castle 30
20. Aerial view of Bodiam Castle 35
21. Internal view of the gatehouse, Bodiam Castle 36
22. Three arches, Bodiam Castle 36
23. Bodiam Castle, 1903, before restoration 37
24. Remains of chapel and Lady's Bower, Bodiam Castle .. 38
25. Surviving wall of the keep, Bramber Castle 40
26. Reconstruction of Bramber Castle, from an old drawing .. 43
27. Aerial view of Camber Castle 44
28. Entrance of the central tower, Camber Castle 46
29. Remains of Chichester Castle 50
30. Restored section of city wall and one of the gateways,
    Chichester 53
31. Remains of entrance front, Cowdray Castle 54
32. Kitchen tower and ruined chapel, Cowdray Castle 56
33. Cowdray Castle 57
34. Print of Cowdray Castle prior to destruction by fire in
    1793 58

35. Ruins of Crowhurst Castle 60
36. Two lancet windows, Crowhurst Castle 63
37. Ruins of the collegiate church, Hastings Castle 64
38. Aerial view of Hastings Castle 66
39. Stump of one of the gatehouse towers, Hastings Castle .. 68
40. Print of Hastings Castle, 1840 71
41. The mound at Hastings Castle 72
42. Entrance front of Herstmonceux Castle 74
43. View of the gatehouse, Herstmonceux Castle 77
44. The double-parapeted gatehouse, Herstmonceux Castle .. 78
45. World war II aerial view of Herstmonceux Castle 79
46. Photograph of 1891 showing Herstmonceux Castle prior
      to restoration 81
47. Remains of a single wall of the keep, Knepp Old Castle .. 84
48. Close-up view of the keep, Knepp Old Castle 86
49. Print of Knepp Old Castle, dated 1776 89
50. Barbican and gatehouse, Lewes Castle 90
51. Aerial view of the mound, Lewes Castle 92
52. The mound and shell keep, Lewes Castle 95
53. Internal view of the shell keep, Lewes Castle 97
54. Petworth House 98
55. A 19th-century engraving of Petworth House 100
56. Looking through an arrow loop, Pevensey Castle 102
57. View of the Roman fort, Pevensey, from an old engraving 104
58. Aerial view of the Roman fort and medieval castle,
      Pevensey 105
59. The Roman westgate, Pevensey Castle 107
60. Internal view of Pevensey Castle 109
61. Pevensey Castle 110
62. The Ypres Tower, Rye 112
63. The Land Gate, Rye 114
64. Rectangular tower at Ypres Tower, Rye 117
65. The 14th-century Strand Gate, Winchelsea 118
66. Entrance passage and vaulting, Strand Gate, Winchelsea .. 121
67. The Gatehouse, Bolebroke Castle 138
68. Eridge Castle, just prior to its destruction 138
69. A 19th-century print of Knepp New Castle 138

LIST OF COLOUR PLATES

I	The Strand Gate at Winchelsea	*facing page* 2
II	The ruins of Pevensey Castle	*facing page* 19
III	Cowdray Castle	*facing page* 19
IV	Herstmonceux Castle	*facing page* 114
V	Arundel Castle	*facing page* 114
VI	Bodiam Castle	*facing page* 131

LIST OF PLANS

The Shoreline at Camber	48
Chichester Castle and City Walls	52
Ruins of Crowhurst Castle	62
Ground plan of Hastings Castle	66
Ground plan of Sedgwick Castle	134

ACKNOWLEDGEMENTS

I should like to express my thanks to Colin Guy for his very excellent series of line drawings and plans. (Some of the marginal illustrations are by Carolyn Lockwood and others were redrawn from M. and C. H. B. Quennell's *A History of Everyday Things in England*, Batsford, 1918.) I am also very grateful to my sister, Susan Hidson, for reading the manuscript and typing it for me.

The prints came from two sources: numbers 23, 26, 46 and 68 were kindly supplied by Elaine Baird of Brighton Reference Library, and numbers 6, 9, 34, 40, 49, 55, 57 and 63 by Mr. Hassell of the East Sussex County Library, Lewes. Numbers 1, 2, 3, 4, 8, 20, 27, 38, 45, 51, and 58 are taken from the Cambridge University Collection (copyright reserved) and are reproduced here with their permission. All of the remaining photographs were taken either by myself of Colin Guy. The map of Camber's changing shoreline is based on one produced by the East Sussex County Council.

Colour photographs nos. I - IV inclusive are by John Guy. No. V is by Rosemary Savage and no. VI is by Ann Hewitt.

My thanks also to Roger Sharplin for his help with my researches; Leonard Hill, Ltd., of Rochester for their photographic services; the staffs of various public libraries, especially to Brighton and Chatham reference libraries, the Public Record Office, British Museum and Cambridge University. The genealogical tables were compiled with the grateful help of Professor Sir David Waldron Smithers and Cliff Hansford. My thanks also to the owners and administrators of all the castles mentioned, especially to the late Baroness Emmet of Amberley Castle.

Finally, I must pay tribute to my family for their continued support, and to my publisher, for giving me the opportunity to write this book, especially to Noel Osborne, Editorial Director, without whose interest and kind help the project might never have got off the ground. My thanks to them all.

Introduction

Sussex possesses a fine collection of fortifications dating from pre-historic times to the present day, including a magnificent array of hillforts and other prehistoric earthworks, and examples from almost every period of castellar construction. The types of fortification we recognise today as castles are well represented and, while they do not number so many as in neighbouring Kent, Sussex certainly possesses some of the most visually attractive castles in England. Moreover, such castles as Cowdray, Herstmonceux and Arundel, and Bodiam in its haunting beauty are, without doubt, amongst the most picturesque and enigmatic in Europe.

To understand what a castle is and what characteristics distinguish it from other types of fortress, it is necessary to know something of the general history of fortification. The first types of fortification known to us are the many hill-top forts of the Iron Age and earlier (*c.* 600 B.C. –*c.* 55 B.C.). In Sussex we have excellent examples at Cissbury, Hollingbury, Chanctonbury and the Devil's Dyke.

However, care should be taken when considering the origins and purpose of hillforts. Some it seems were intentionally built for defensive purposes, others were hastily put into some sort of defensive condition as protection, albeit ineffective in the event, against the invading Roman legions. A large number of prehistoric earthworks, however, may not have been fortresses at all, though we usually combine them under the general heading of hillforts. Many of them may simply have been enclosed camps, farmsteads, village communities, or livestock compounds. However, this somewhat controversial subject is beyond the scope of this book, so cannot be dealt with here.

A number, at least, were hillforts. Their general characteristics are more-or-less common throughout, and consist of a large levelled area, usually on top of a hill, with the sides scarped all round to form a series of steep banks and ditches. Embankments and timber (sometimes stone) ramparts were carried around the perimeter presenting what must have been a very formidable obstacle. The basic methods of constructing the ditches and embankments were still used in the later fortifications of the Middle Ages and formed as important a part of the defences as the walls afterwards built upon them.

Hillforts were built for communal defence; so, too, were the Roman fortifications that followed, either to enclose a town or a military camp. Saxon England saw the rise of burghs, or fortified townships —again for communal use. Towards the end of the Saxon period, however, there began to appear a new type of defence system—the fortification of private dwellings. It either evolved simultaneously with a similar system on the Continent, or was influenced by it at a very early date. At any rate it received its greatest impetus under the Normans who can claim to have advanced its principles, if not actually to have invented them. The system was the feudal system, and the private fortifications came to be known as castles.

The basic principle of the feudal system was that all land ultimately belonged to the king, large parcels of which were let out to sub-tenants —the barons. They divided the land again into individual manors, which in turn were sub-let. All the key areas were controlled by the private fortified residences of the barons, with the king in overall command. The local population would help to man these defences on a rota basis, known as 'castle guard'. Collectively they formed part of the national defence system, but individually they were the private houses of their owners. This, then, is the most distinctive feature of a castle from other forms of defensive building—it was a private fortress. Later, castles came to protect the communities they commanded, but they retained until the end the basic principle of being a private fortress.

1. Selham Castle. An aerial view showing the earthwork remains of Selham, an early motte-and-bailey castle.

I. The Strand Gate at Winchelsea.

Such a system was instrumental in helping Duke William to control his newly-conquered dominions in England. When a more settled environment allowed, castles were used to protect England from subsequent invasion, for any would-be conqueror had first to control the castles. Castles became key factors in medieval politics and life, but their purpose has been somewhat misunderstood in recent years. Too much emphasis has been placed upon their military roles and far too little upon the more important role of acting in an administrative capacity.

The first castles to be built in England by the Normans were of a type now known as motte and bailey castles. They consisted usually of a mound of earth, surrounded by a ditch, connected to a levelled area, or courtyard, similarly ditched all round to connect to that around the base of the mound, thus forming a continuous figure-of-eight moat. An earthen rampart was formed around the perimeter of the courtyard and also round the top of the mound to enclose another small courtyard, surmounted by a timber palisade. A tower was then erected within this enclosure on top of the mound, and various domestic apartments built within the larger enclosure, afterwards known as the bailey.

2. Aerial view of Bramber Castle showing the central mound and the surviving fragment of the keep. The earthworks are obscured by trees; note the parish church immediately beside the castle, to the left of the picture.

3. Aerial view showing the saucer shaped mound and moat, Knepp Old Castle.

Early examples were usually built from timber, but as soon as time and money allowed the defences were replaced in stone. In Sussex there are many excellent examples of motte and bailey castles, including Bramber and Knepp. But the two finest examples are Fulking, which is now devoid of all masonry and shows perfectly the basic outline, and the magnificent Arundel castle which shows how they developed from such humble beginnings to the mighty buildings we see today.

4. Aerial view of Arundel Castle showing perfectly the layout of the castle with its central mound and two baileys.

At the heart of every motte and bailey castle is a mound. The Bayeux tapestry shows workmen busily erecting (or apparently so) a mound at Hastings, and it has long been assumed that the Normans built all the mounds for their castles. The author's recent researches and those of other writers, however, have cast a new light upon the origins of castle earthworks. [In the writer's *Kent Castles* will be found extensive notes relating to them, a summary of which appears below.] The speed with which many Norman castles were erected first aroused my interest in the study of their earthworks. It seems that the Normans almost always made use of any feature that already existed, be it natural or man-made, and used it as the nucleus for one of their motte and bailey castles. A small hill or rise in the general level of the surrounding land were obvious attractions. By scarping the sides of the hill a mound could easily be formed, which was supplemented by ditches and banks.

However, scattered across the British landscape is an incredible number of isolated mounds of prehistoric date—an estimated 40,000 in England alone. Some of them were burial mounds, but the vast majority are of unknown purpose. Not originally intended for defensive purposes, they formed the ideal nucleus for many a Norman motte and bailey. Excavation of many sites has often proved their more ancient origins.

Many sites are of entirely Norman construction, but all received appropriate modifications by them. This in no way undermines the ingenuity and obvious tactical skill of the Normans in erecting so many castles so quickly, thus securing an early and permanent conquest of England. Indeed, it serves only to accentuate their inventiveness in recognising the potential of such ancient sites. I hesitate to suggest that such prehistoric mounds were the inspiration for the unique shape of fortification known as a motte and bailey, but it is not impossible. Once established, castles developed at a rapid pace, some-times following the shapes of the earlier motte and bailey structures, sometimes entirely separate from them.

While many historians would like to believe that the development of medieval castles followed a smooth, logical pattern, the reality is somewhat different. Unlike fortifications erected by such as the Romans, who tended to choose sites capable of supporting their rigidly symmetrical forts, the shape of a castle was dictated by its site. Thus most castles are of irregular shape, often following the contours of the land. This, coupled with the very important factor that they were each held privately, tended to give a free-hand for each castle to develop separately. At each site today, what we see is not a universal develop-ment common to all castles, but a highly individual development.

Each castle developed according to the limitations of its site and the time and money available to its owners. Castles held by the king or by the leading barons tended to be much grander, simply because more money was available. Those held by minor lords developed at a slower pace, their owners being more satisfied with the defences their castles already possessed, rather than continually to up-date them. We therefore find at all castles a mixture of architectural styles and defence techniques dating from all periods of the Middle Ages.

A large number of castles were built in the early years after the Conquest, particularly during the troubled reign of Stephen, when they mushroomed all over the country. This random process was checked by Henry II, that most able of kings, who brought castle building under strict royal control. He destroyed many of the adulterine, or unlicensed, castles that had been built without royal permission, and seized control of all the more important ones, installing in them his trusted supporters as constables. Further, he decreed that all new castles, or the refortification of existing ones, could only be constructed by royal licence—i.e., 'licence to crenellate'.

The hey-day of the English castle was between the years 1066–1485, reaching a peak during the reign of Edward I. His mammoth castle building programme, particularly in Wales, carried the principles of castellar construction to their absolute zenith. Such castles as Caernarfon, Conwy and Beaumaris are justifiably considered to be the finest ever built. After Edward's time changing methods of warfare and in social structures rendered the castle more-or-less obsolete as a form of defence. Castle design reverted to a more basic and less formidable plan. The courtyard-type castle, of which Bodiam is indisputably the finest, came into its own.

The function of these later castles was not to hold down a newly-conquered territory, nor to control and command a region, but to provide protection for a lord and his army (which now comprised hired mercenaries instead of the local population serving castle guard) or a place to retire to between forays on the field. Guns were introduced into castle designs at this time, seen in the key-hole shape loops in the walls (e.g., Bodiam), but they had little effect upon the decline of castles, whose days were by then numbered as viable pieces in war-mongering games, for battles were decided on the field rather than by the taking and holding of castles. The death knell of the castle was sounded not by the development of artillery, but by the break-up of the feudal system itself, which created and sustained it.

Castles, although instrumental in the politics of their day, were very rarely called upon to do battle, for they are, by nature, passive and were built more for their deterrent value than as instruments of war.

Once built, a castle's existence was usually sufficient to guarantee a peaceful career. It is often forgotten that they were the seats of local administration and revenue collection points, and the resident lords were far more interested in the day-to-day running of their attendant manors than in war. Their owners and contents had necessarily to be protected, but that is not to say their defences were continually put to the test. In fact, the opposite is true, for on the comparatively few occasions they were called in to service, they had to be repaired hurriedly and made ready.

In short, full-scale sieges were very costly affairs, both in terms of money and loss of life, and no baron would lightly indulge in one. Treaties and exchanges of property were invariably conducted on paper in preference to fighting. Proof of this relative inactivity can be shown in two ways. Firstly, the study of an average castle for the entire period of its active life, say from 1100 to 1500, will reveal comparatively few incidents recorded against it. Even allowing for missing records, one or two sieges would be considered more than average, three well above average, while none is more normal. Many castles only ever saw action during the 17th-century Civil War, and then for quite different reasons.

Our view of the Middle Ages has been grossly distorted by the romance of such tales as Sir Walter Scott's *Ivanhoe*. We have been led to believe that castles were armed to the teeth at all times in readiness for a siege, but the truth is opposite. As for the tales of dungeons, we might imagine all castles to have more wretches incarcerated in their prisons than numbered the entire castle household. Few castles actually had a dungeon, most using a small room as a prison cell—more likely for the confinement of those who could not pay their taxes and fines than for the extraction of secrets from political prisoners. Violence and atrocities were certainly committed during the Middle Ages, but probably no more then than they are now. It is one thing for the Tower of London to have witnessed untold horrors at the hands of tyrannical kings, but it is quite different to expect all castles to have done so.

The second factor to bear out the relative military inactivity of castles is the high standard of living carried on within them. We often assume the inhabitants of castles to have been crude, dirty and uncivilised, an assumption kindled perhaps by the grimness of castle ruins today. We seem completely to have overlooked that many hundreds of years of neglect and deliberate destruction have robbed their walls of all decoration. Castle interiors were very much more comfortable than we might imagine, and included such luxuries as flush toilets, running water, brightly-painted walls and, in some extreme cases, double glazing. A far cry indeed from the popular conception of a castle.

If such a level of domesticity existed inside castles—and there is evidence that it did at most of them—then no baron in his right mind would want to see its deliberate destruction in a siege unless absolutely necessary. A brief study of the expenditure accounts of even the royal castles bears this out, for money spent on the interior fittings and decoration far outweighs that spent on matters of defence. One begins to wonder if the elaborate and sophisticated interiors of such reconstructed castles as Arundel are not perhaps a little nearer to what castles actually looked like in their day than we are generally prepared to accept.

Following the decline of the medieval castle, castle building saw a brief revival under Henry VIII when he feared reprisals from France and Germany after his departure from the Catholic faith. Strictly speaking they were not castles at all, not being the private fortresses of feudal lords but essentially military blockhouses. They housed a small garrison and had large-bore cannons mounted on enormously thick bastions and walls, designed primarily for defence of the coast. They still show sufficient similarity to medieval castles, however, to warrant the title 'castle'. Camber is the only example in Sussex, a splendid symmetrically designed fort still in very good condition.

5. Camber Castle viewed from the north-west, showing the entrance through one of the bastions.

After the Tudor period, the two basic elements of the feudal castle —house and fortress—went their separate ways. Houses built after that time, although often perpetuating architectural features common to castles, were not defensible buildings, but merely continued the style from a combined sense of tradition and prestige. Structures built for defensive purposes again became the entire responsibility of the state and contained only the meanest of apartments to house the garrison.

The decline of the castle and subsequent rise of the stately home gradually evolved over a period of time. Buildings belonging to this transitional stage in Sussex are Herstmonceux and Cowdray castles, two of the finest examples of their type ever built. While they are primarily houses in their overall design, the elements of feudalism have not been entirely lost and they still preserve many genuine features of defence in the form of drawbridges, moats and gun-loops.

6. Eridge Castle, from a 19th-century lithograph, showing the splendid proportions of this fairy-tale 'sham' castle.

Finally, after many years spent in the shadows, Gothic building styles were revived in the 18th and 19th centuries, and along with them a revival in castle building. These castles were very different from genuine castles, however, and were built partly for social prestige—many of the new breed of 'aristocracy' (mainly industrialists) desired a fitting residence (and what could be more suitable than a castle?)— and partly as a result of the romantic revival of medievalism. Sir Walter Scott and other writers led the revival, and while they are undoubtedly guilty of distorting the true colour of the period, they did at least revive an interest that is present still and might otherwise have lain dormant. Many of the castles built in the 'Mock Gothick' style, as it came to be termed, are outrageously extravagant, but they make no pretext to be castles proper and should be enjoyed for their own sakes. Included among them in Sussex are the splendid Castle Goring and Knepp New Castle.

This brief introduction to castle building, its motivations and reasons for decline, cannot claim to capture the full story, but it is hoped that sufficient details have been supplied for the reader to approach the following individual histories of Sussex castles with a better understanding. The pastime of castle visiting is increasingly more popular and I cannot recommend too strongly a visit to each of the castles described.

7. The splendid entrance front, Castle Goring.

In this book certain criteria have been adopted: to keep within the confines of the title all, or at least most, of those buildings now known as 'castles'—Roman fort, medieval castle, Henrician blockhouse, or Victorian folly—have been described. There was not room for the earlier fortifications of the Iron Age, Saxon or Danish periods, nor for the semi-fortified abbeys, church towers and manor houses. This study claims neither to be definitive nor exhaustive, but I hope it will be enjoyed by novice and enthusiast alike for its own sake.

Castles in Sussex

8. An aerial view of Amberley Castle.

Amberley

(Aumberle. Amberle. From amber, a measure, or Eanburg, the lea or meadow of Eanburg.)

Amberley castle is one of the loveliest castles in the south of England, and also one of the least known. It stands partly ruined, partly restored to a habitable residence, overlooking a beautiful stretch of marshland and water meadows of the river Arun known as the Wild Brooks. In the time of the Emmets' ownership they kindly gave me access to the castle ruins, which form a delightful garden to the house and are still completely enclosed within the outer curtain wall.

The castle is a fortified manor house of the bishops of Chichester and surprisingly little is known of its history. The original site of Chichester cathedral was at Selsey, until 1070, when the encroaching sea brought about its collapse. St Wilfrid was granted lands at Amberley in 861 by King Cedwalla and some 400 years later Bishop Luffa, who also rebuilt Chichester cathedral, built a manor house and church there. The first house was not fortified and much of it survives today. It stands now in the south-east corner of the present castle and formed the principal living accommodation. Its close association with successive bishops accounts for the fact that the parish church is immediately adjacent to the castle. There was also a small chapel in the house, and later castle, built out of part of the old hall range and now included in the present living apartments; the piscina survives as do some of the old windows.

The house was surrounded by the present strong curtain wall following a licence to crenellate of 10 December 1377. It was built by Bishop William Rede at a time when England was experiencing political and social unrest, and suffering lightning raids by the French. The river Arun was navigable as far as Arundel (as it still is) which made the bishop's house at Amberley very vulnerable to attack. The Church, as an institution, had been singled out by the populace as one of the rich oppressors and suffered greatly as a result. The Lollards, we may remember, were active at the time and a few years later Archbishop Sudbury was murdered by the 'mob' at Canterbury.

The castle Bishop Rede built was roughly rectangular, but the north wall bulged at its eastern end to form an almost rhomboid shape. It

13

9. A 19th-century print of Amberley Castle by I. Higham, showing the impressive gatehouse prior to restoration.

was furnished with a fine twin-towered gatehouse, complete with drawbridge and portcullis—but no machicolations above the gateway as was normal for the period. The only external extensions to an otherwise plain wall face are a small garderobe tower and a kitchen block. There were towers at each corner but these projected internally and for that reason may have been added at a later date. This is a serious flaw from a military point of view because the towers thus could not provide flanking fire along the curtain walls.

The surrounding curtain wall is very high—about 40ft. in places—and the towers would probably have risen a little higher than that. The garderobe tower is the best preserved and contains two of the finest latrines to have survived from the Middle Ages. The latrine shafts are thrown across the external angles of the tower in the form of two arches—an arrangement that I have not come across at any other castle. The south side of the castle was protected by a moat, but the marshland of the Wild Brooks gave ample protection on the north side.

Bishop Rede extended the original manor house and added a great hall, separate apartments for guests and retainers, and a complete suite of rooms along the north and south curtain walls, their positions marked today by fireplaces, corbels for roof supports and joist holes.

10. Amberley Castle: the arches springing from each side of the garderobe tower carry two latrine shafts, a somewhat unusual feature. Note also the gun and arrow loops.

Ironically, most of his buildings (excluding the curtain wall) lie in ruins and what survives dates mostly from the earlier manor house. The outer wall remains virtually intact (except for the loss of its parapet), as does the now-restored, magnificent outer gatehouse. A smaller water-gate or postern also survives in the west wall.

Amberley castle seems to have been much favoured by the bishops of Chichester, and Bishop Rede signed many of his documents whilst in residence there. There is believed to have been a prison somewhere in the castle, for a certain William Fretton, a clerk from Coombes, was imprisoned there on 16 May 1415 for committing a felony. In its later history a court room was set up in part of the hall block, where many local cases and disputes were settled.

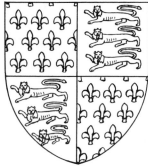

The castle remained virtually unaltered until Bishop Sherburne received a second licence to crenellate in the early 16th century. He seems not to have acted on this, however, but some improvements were made to the house, particularly to the Queen's Room and to the internal decorations. A number of painted panels were inserted in the 13th-century hall at this time, depicting the 'Heroines of Antiquity' and various other mythological figures. Eight of the original nine panels still survive in the house, along with a later 17th-century panel, and together they form a unique and special part of Amberley's decorations. Bishop Sherbourne spent a great deal of time at Amberley, but subsequent bishops seem to have preferred their other episcopal seat at

11. The west front of Amberley Castle from the adjacent farmyard. Note the postern door half-way up the wall.

Aldingbourne. After the Dissolution, Amberley ceased to be lived in by bishops and was then leased to various tenants.

In 1538 the castle was let to Sir William Shelley and Sir William Goring at an annual rent of £73 8s. 0d. The house seems still to have been maintained in good repair, for in 1577 we hear of Elizabeth Earnley of Cakeham giving birth to a son, Edward, who was baptized by Thomas Sadler in the castle chapel. After the Shelleys' and Gorings' occupation, who kept the tenancy until 1578, the Lewknors moved in under Robert Lewknor. The Lewknors, Shelleys and Gorings, however, were very closely involved with one another's affairs and frequently members of all three families were in residence throughout the Lewknor tenancy. In 1643, during the Civil War, John Goring was in residence. He was a staunch royalist and it is thought likely that the castle was dismantled at this time by General Sir William Waller.

Goring was renowned for obstructing payment of taxes to parliament and tried to persuade the people of Amberley to bring all their goods and valuables into the castle. Such an act would have been construed by parliament as siding with the royalist cause and it is not certain whether the townspeople agreed to Goring's request or not. Goring continued to obstruct parliament and installed himself at Amberley in readiness for a siege. It became necessary for General Waller to march over from Arundel castle, which he had recently taken, to wrest Goring from Amberley and seize his possessions and back taxes. It is unlikely that Waller mounted a full-scale siege against Amberley—the outer walls certainly show no signs of heavy bombardment—but he did effect an entry, seize John Goring and wreck the internal buildings of the castle. Thomas Lewknor, the then owner, was fined £84 for this inconvenience in 1649, but the previous year the castle had already been confiscated by parliament, along with other church property, and sold to John Butler for £3,341 14s. 4d.

John Goring was unrepentant and remained rebellious to the end, for in 1648, the year of the Sussex insurrection, he is reputed to have '. . . desired to ride with arms to Lord Goring of Portsmouth, and promised him great rewards if the King's forces should prevail against Parliament, telling him he would be a Colonel in the King's army; and that half a year ago John Goring had drunk a toaste to Prince Charles and the confusion of Parliament'.

From the Butlers, Amberley passed to Sir James Brisco, the Parkers, Sir James Peachey, and various other notable families, including the Harwoods who established a farmyard within its walls, until it was purchased in 1893 by the Duke of Norfolk. In 1908 the 15th Duke undertook the repair of the castle walls and restored the gatehouse to its present condition. The castle was purchased in 1925 by Thomas

12. Looking along the north front of Amberley Castle towards the garderobe tower, from across the Wild Brooks, a delightful area of unspoilt marshland.

II. The ruins of Pevensey Castle.

III. Cowdray Castle.

Emmet who, the following year, restored the house and made it once more a habitable residence. In 1964 his widow, Baroness Emmet, was made a life peeress and she lived at Amberley until her recent death in the autumn of 1980. She was a charming lady and never turned interested visitors away from her door, even though the castle is not normally open to the public, and will be sadly missed by all who knew her. I personally shall remember her for the invaluable help she gave me with my researches and for the splendid way in which she kept Amberley castle.

Baroness Emmet opened the castle gardens to the public each Easter, under the National Gardens Scheme, an ideal opportunity to inspect the castle courtyard. Much of the exterior can be seen from the village, the Wild Brooks and from the adjoining churchyard. The village itself, almost entirely thatched, is highly picturesque, and slumbers away at the foot of the castle walls. Because it is so little known, even though Arundel—to which Amberley castle was once supposed to have been connected by a secret passage—is only five miles away, nothing disturbs this wholly tranquil scene. Were the castle not the picturesque ruin it now is, one might be excused for thinking Amberley to have been caught in time, frozen in the far-off days of the Middle Ages, a feeling which cannot but add to its obvious romantic appeal.

13. View from the surrounding park showing the magnificent 19th-century reconstruction work on Arundel Castle in detail.

Arundel

(Harundel. Arundelle. Har-hun-dell, hoarhound valley or hirondelle, a swallow.)

> 'Oft on the mouldering keep by night
> Earl Roger takes his stand,
> With the sword that shone at Hastings' fight,
> Firm grasped in his red, right hand!'

So begins an old poem about Roger Montgomery who fought alongside Duke William at Hastings and was richly rewarded for his services. William bestowed upon him the earldoms of Shrewsbury and Arundel, of which the latter included the Rape and Honour of that district. Roger also founded the abbey at Shrewsbury, which he entered as a monk just three days before his death. His ghost is reputed to linger on at Arundel, where it haunts the keep.

Earl Roger built the first castle at Arundel, but a great deal of what the visitor sees today is the result of 18th- and 19th-century reconstruction. The castle has suffered harsh criticism as a result of this reconstruction, most of it unjustly so I feel, particularly the comments of Ian Nairn who proclaims it to be 'a great disappointment' from the moment one enters the gates. I disagree most strongly with this, and other such comments, and feel that they have rather missed the point. It is currently fashionable to criticise all Victorian attempts at recreating Gothic architecture without regard for the obvious skills involved in designing and erecting such buildings. It is frequently forgotten that while some original work has been swept away, very often there would be nothing left to us if the Victorians had not taken them in hand, since many buildings had suffered long years of neglect. Were not the medieval builders themselves guilty of such sweeping rebuilding programmes, for how many of the buildings of the Middle Ages are datable to one period?

Another criticism levelled against the Victorians is their interpretation of medieval interiors. While they may be guilty of handing on a rather false image of the past, in certain respects it seems they may have had a better idea of the interior of castles than we have. My extensive research into this subject reveals that castles were substantially more comfortable inside than our previous assumption that castles were always grim, cold and foreboding would indicate. The time has come to review Victorian-Gothic interiors in a new light. I do not claim that the Victorians correctly interpreted medieval art and culture at all levels, but they have been unjustly criticised for their attempt.

Arundel castle is a masterpiece and fast becoming a monument to the achievements of the Victorian era. The beauty of its interior has often been overlooked from concern for the original work that was replaced, but it is unsurpassed and deserves now to be regarded in its own right. The craftsmanship of the Victorian work is superb, comparable even to that of the Middle Ages. I believe the Victorians themselves have been misunderstood in this respect. My own view is that they were not trying to recreate the Middle Ages, but rather to use it as a source of inspiration on which to base their own art. They deliberately extended the principles of Gothic architecture, not from ignorance, but as a genuine attempt to develop the style to its absolute limit, mixing all forms of it together to create a romantic whole. Their ideal perhaps was that if the Middle Ages were not really as they saw them, then they should have been for the sake of romance. They came remarkably close to achieving that ideal at Arundel.

The origins of Arundel castle are more obscure than its later history. Tradition asserts that King Alfred had a fortress here, though not a castle, and a character named Bevis, a giant, is also reputed to have built some kind of defences on the site. There is no supportive evidence for either of these claims, however, save for an epic poem written about Bevis at an unknown date by an unknown author—hardly authentication for any story. He is supposed still to haunt the castle keep, suggested by the following lines from the poem:

'... there, 'tis said, mid scenes forlorn,
When Midnight spreads her dreamy pall,
The blast of Bevis' bugle horn
Rings loudly from its ramparts tall.'

A mound in the castle park is, by popular tradition, the burial place of this Bevis, whose name has been perpetuated in the Bevis Tower, a medieval structure standing close to the keep.

It is with the arrival of Earl Roger de Montgomery that Arundel castle enters the realm of historical fact. The first castle he built was of the motte and bailey type and of timber construction. It is a classic example of a motte and bailey with a large central mound and two baileys, an hour-glass shape reminiscent of Windsor castle. Earl Roger soon began the replacement of Arundel's defences in stone, and dating from his time are the keep and at least part of the Bevis Tower, erected between 1070-90. Fragments of his curtain wall also survive within the present structure. Very much more of Arundel's original walls still

14.   The upper ward, Arundel Castle, showing the Bevis tower; restored, but of medieval construction.

15.   The magnificent shell keep crowning the mound at Arundel. Note the original entrance door-way to the right of the keep.

survives, despite all the later rebuilding, than might be imagined, but you have to look for it. Many walls are no longer visible, encased within the core of later walls, but they are nevertheless still there.

First granted to Roger de Montgomery in 1067, the castle afterwards passed to his son, Hugh, who died without issue leaving it to his brother, Robert de Belesme. He rebelled, unsuccessfully, against Henry I who attacked and took Arundel castle, and as a result Belesme forfeited his estates to the crown. The king held them directly for a short while, but then he granted them to William de Albini, investing in him also the titles Earl of Arundel and Chief Butler of England. William married Henry I's widow, Adeliza of Louvain, in 1138, and the following year invited the dead king's daughter, Matilda, to stay at Arundel.

After the tragedy of the 'White Ship', in which Henry I's son and heir was drowned, the king made his barons swear allegiance to Matilda as heir to the throne on his death. Many barons supported the king's nephew, Stephen, who was in the event crowned king, and England was thrown into the conflicts of a bloody civil war to resolve the dispute. After many changes of fortune it was agreed that Stephen should remain on the throne, but on his death Matilda's son Henry would be crowned king, so ending direct Norman rule and introducing a new line into the English monarchy, the Plantagenets.

Matilda stayed at Arundel in a room still called 'Queen Matilda's Room', over the gatehouse leading to the keep. Stephen arrived with a large army to besiege the castle but was unable to gain entry. Afterwards, Matilda fled to the West Country where she was eventually taken prisoner and escorted to Bristol castle. Arundel castle remained in de Albini hands, passing successively to three more earls all named William. The last in the family line, Hugh de Albini, 5th Earl of Arundel, died young in 1243 leaving no heir. The estates were then divided, and John Fitzalan of Clun, who had married Hugh's daughter Isabel, acquired the Castle and Honour of Arundel. The Fitzalans held the castle in an almost uninterrupted line until 1555 when Mary Fitzalan, the last of the family, married Thomas, 4th Duke of Norfolk, thus carrying Arundel into the Howard family—who still own it. The castle and title, Duke of Norfolk, became the most powerful and influential in the land, particularly during the Tudor regime.

Richard Fitzalan was created Earl of Arundel in 1290 and was responsible for much building work at the castle, including the barbican which stands today in front of the old Norman gatehouse. He fought alongside Edward I at the siege of Caerlaverock castle in 1300 and was bestowed with many honours. Not so fortunate was his son Edmund, however, who was beheaded in 1326 for his part in the rebellion against Edward II. Arundel passed briefly to the Earl of Kent, 6th son of Edward I, but when he himself was beheaded four years later the castle was returned to the Fitzalans.

Richard Fitzalan, 3rd Earl, who took part in the battle of Crecy, added the estates of the de Warenne family to those of Arundel when his uncle, the Earl of Surrey, died. His son, another Richard, is remembered for his supposed treachery to King Richard II. He began by actively supporting the king, but afterwards changed sides and was duly executed. As a result, Richard II confiscated Arundel and granted it to his loyal friend John Holland, Duke of Exeter. The estates were restored to the Fitzalans under Henry IV when Thomas Fitzalan was given the added distinction of being made a Knight of the Garter. Another member of the family created a Knight of the Garter was William Fitzalan, 9th Earl, who also served as Governor of Dover castle and Warden of the Cinque Ports. All the Fitzalans became soldiers or courtiers of distinction, and Arundel frequently played host to visiting royalty.

The outer gatehouse and barbican of Arundel Castle contains much ginal work, and still shows signs of Waller's bombardment in 1643/4 ring the Civil War.

Of the Howard family one member in particular, Thomas, 3rd Duke of Norfolk, deserves special mention for the role he played in the complex and often dangerous politics of Henry VIII's court. An unscrupulous, power-hungry man, his importance challenged even that of King Henry himself. To increase his influence at court he connived to marry off two of his nieces to Henry—Anne Boleyn, the king's second wife, and Katherine Howard, his fifth wife. Both ladies were ruthlessly exploited by their uncle and sadly ended their lives on the block. Thomas made no attempt to prevent their executions, for fear of reprisals from the king, and even tried to marry his own daughter Mary into the royal family. She married Henry's illegitimate son, Henry Fitzroy, Duke of Richmond, but he died before the marriage could be consummated. Thomas's son was executed on a trumped-up charge of laying claim to the throne and himself only avoided execution by the premature death of Henry VIII on the day before sentence was due to be pronounced. His grandson, 4th Duke, was executed by Elizabeth I in 1572 because he had the misfortune to fall in love with Mary Queen of Scots. It was his marriage in 1555 to Lady Mary Fitzalan that had united the two great families of Fitzalan and Howard.

The Howard's fortunes not surprisingly dwindled following this disastrous chain of events and the dukedom was attainted. The estates were partially restored to Thomas, 14th Earl of Arundel, but not the dukedom. He was a patron of the arts and amassed a fine collection of paintings. Gradually he built up the family fortunes once more. At the outbreak of the Civil War he left England temporarily to reside abroad, and it was whilst he was out of the country that Arundel entered its bleakest period. The castle was held for the royalists during the war and was attacked by General Sir William Waller between 20 December 1643 and 6 January 1644. The siege was devastating, cannons even being mounted on the tower of the parish church to fire down into the castle courtyard. The events of the siege have been fully recorded and so great was the damage caused that 'the roofless apartments were left to moulder in neglect or sink beneath the ravages of the elements'. And so the castle remained until the mid-18th century.

Thomas, 16th Earl, was restored to the title Duke of Norfolk in 1660 by Charles II, but no longer did he or any subsequent dukes play so prominent a part in English politics. The 8th Duke intended building a new house at Arundel, but contented himself with repairing the south range of the castle in 1716; he faced it with brick which has since been removed. Further repairs to the house, but not to the castle itself, were carried out in subsequent years, but in 1787 the

11th Duke, Charles Howard, an amateur architect on friendly terms with the Prince Regent, decided completely to reconstruct the castle to his own designs. Work was completed in 1815 at the cost of an incredible £600,000.

Queen Victoria stayed at Arundel in 1846 (her bed is still shown to visitors), but the castle she saw is not the one we see today. Henry Granville, 14th Duke, began to reconstruct the castle again, this time to the designs of M. E. Hadfield, but he died before completion. His son Henry, 15th Duke completed the task having chosen C. A. Buckler, a learned antiquary, as his architect, and together they rebuilt Arundel between 1875-1900. Many of the interior features of the previous reconstruction were kept, such as the Barons' Hall, which was formally opened on 15 June 1815 with a magnificent banquet. The castle is still in the hands of the Dukes of Norfolk (though they no longer live there) and is cared for by a trust.

17. View of the reconstructed state apartments at Arundel from within the lower bailey.

18. The barbican towers of the outer gatehouse of Arundel Castle seen from the top of the castle mound.

The stately splendour of Arundel castle interior defies adequate description; how does one 'describe' a work of art? The two most outstanding features of the 'new' castle, however, are the chapel, of almost cathedral-like proportions, and the Barons' Hall, a magnificent chamber 133ft. long and 50ft. high. The roof is singularly beautiful. It is of hammer-beam construction in Spanish chestnut and was inspired by the roof of the Great Hall at Penshurst Place in Kent. The whole castle recently (1975-78) underwent an extensive restoration programme and is now rendered sound for many years to come.

Of the older portions of the castle to be seen the keep is undoubtedly the finest. It preserves at its core the original Norman walls, but most of the present structure dates from 1120-40, though it has been restored. The mound upon which it stands is 230ft. in diameter at the base and varies between 50-70ft. in height, with the keep, itself some 60-70ft. across internally, rising 30ft. above that. The keep is of the type known as a shell keep, the internal buildings originally being lean-tos erected around a central courtyard. A breathtaking view of the castle, the surrounding park and town and countryside beyond can be had from the battlements, where one can better appreciate its strategic importance on the tidal river Arun. (Arun is a back-formation of the word Arundel, the original name of the river being Trent or Tarrant, preserved as Tarrant Street in the town today.)

Before the restoration of the keep, which was for long deliberately left in ruin for its picturesque effect, a colony of owls was kept inside it, with a net strung over the top to form a large aviary. The owls became quite famous and grew to enormous size. A number of them were preserved on their deaths, and one or two stuffed examples are exhibited in the castle today. A tradition exists at the castle that when someone in the family is about to die, a white owl is seen fluttering desperately at one of the windows.

19. The impressive entrance front at Bodiam, showing the central gatehouse.

Bodiam

(Bodeham. Bodiham. Boda's Ham.)

Bodiam castle was aptly described by Lord Curzon of Kedleston as 'the most fairy' of English castles, and few who have seen it will disagree. It epitomises the romantic, 'dream' castle of everyone's imagination, yet comparatively few of its type were actually built. Its 'type' can more accurately be described as a courtyard castle, with the various apartments arranged around a central court. It was frequently the case for a lord in the late 14th century to hire a regular retainer of mercenary soldiers instead of relying on the old feudal system of castle guard. Mercenaries were not always to be trusted, for with money as their only master they could, and frequently did, switch loyalties to suit their own ends.

Castles built during this period, the last true castles to be built in England, were provided with completely separate suites of rooms for the lord, his domestic retainers, guests, and the garrison. The lord was thus able to hold his part of the castle against his own mercenary soldiers should the need arise, particularly as he usually controlled the gatehouse as well. Bodiam was appointed in this way, and the lord's apartments are clearly distinguishable from the others. The need for such precautionary measures never arose at Bodiam, however, for the castle was never attacked—except for the briefest of skirmishes during the 17th-century Civil War, the details of which are still not absolutely clear.

As it now stands, beautifully and immaculately preserved with the splendour of its walls mirrored in its lily-decked moat of lake-like proportions, it is hard to visualise anyone actually wanting to attack it. Time, however, has obscured the circumstances leading to its construction, and the countryside then was very different from what we see today. Built by a veteran of the Hundred Years' War, it was intended to protect the then navigable river Rother and halt the piratical raids of the French. The Sussex coastline at that time rendered the entire south-eastern corner of the county very vulnerable to attack. In 1377 Rye and Winchelsea were sacked and burned. Hastings

was attacked in 1380, and in the following years raids increased in both frequency and ferocity.

In answer to these sudden raids Richard II gave to Sir Edward Dalyngrigge a licence to crenellate his house, to protect the inland reaches of the Rother and halt the French advances. Dalyngrigge decided completely to rebuild his house nearer the river to gain better command of its waters. The result is the beautiful Bodiam castle. By the time it was completed, however, the tide of war had turned again in favour of the English, so the castle was never called upon to prove its worth.

Dalyngrigge was something of a character in his day, a soldier of fortune who amassed a great deal of booty from the spoils of the French wars. He was possibly more guilty of piracy and pillage than the French raiders he was commanded to keep out of England. With Sir John Etchingham and Roger de Ashburnham he became a Conservator of the Peace in Kent and Sussex. Immediately after the wave of sackings in 1377, Ashburnham fortified his manor at Scotney, which was then in Sussex but is now in Kent after 19th-century boundary changes. Scotney castle was rhomboid-shaped with four corner towers and a gatehouse in the middle of the south-west side, and the internal rooms were arranged around a central courtyard. Further round the coast at Cooling, overlooking the Thames marshes in Kent, Sir John de Cobham received a licence to crenellate his house there in 1380. The result was the magnificent Cooling castle, similar to Scotney, but containing two independent courtyards separated by a moat. Amberley castle, near Arundel, was also considerably strengthened in about 1377.

When Sir Edward Dalyngrigge received his licence to crenellate on 21 October 1385 he embodied elements of all these castles, combining the better parts into the designs for Bodiam. Scotney and the inner ward at Cooling castle bear a remarkably strong resemblance to Bodiam, but they are surpassed by the sheer strength and grandeur of the latter. It has frequently been said that Dalyngrigge used as his models for Bodiam two continental castles at Derval and Villandraut, which he had seen during his French campaigns, but architectural styles of castles were changing universally, and we need look no further than England for Bodiam's counterparts and source of inspiration.

The early history of Bodiam, until the time of the castle's erection, is obscure and even afterwards is not well documented. Lord Curzon brought together, for the first time, all the information about Bodiam in his book *Bodiam Castle,* published in 1926, and it is largely as a result of his excellent researches that we know so much about it today. The village and manor lie close to the Kent Ditch, the boundary between the two neighbouring counties, but whereas Scotney fell prey to the boundary bureaucrats, Bodiam has fortunately remained in Sussex.

During their occupation of these islands the Romans built a small harbour on the Rother for the export of iron ore extracted nearby. This remained in use until the river was no longer navigable. Both Romano-British and Saxon settlements existed at Bodiam, but little is known about them. The Domesday Survey records Ælfer as holding a moated hall there from the time of Edward the Confessor, which afterwards passed to the Norman son of Hugh d'Eu, Osbernon Osbert. He took the name de Bodeham for his surname. It then passed by marriage to the Wardeux family and so to the Dalyngrigges by the marriage in 1383 of Sir Edward to Elizabeth Wardeux, heiress to the estate in the absence of a direct male line. The Dalyngrigges were an old-established Sussex family whose seat was at Dalling Ridge, near East Grinstead, whence they derived their name.

Sir Edward Dalyngrigge was one of the Royal Commissioners who concluded peace with France, and in 1392 he was appointed Keeper of the Tower of London and Governor of the City. He died in about 1395. His son, John Dalyngrigge, succeeded to the estate and, like his father, was a great favourite at Court and was sent on many missions for the king. On one occasion he escorted Princess Blanche, Henry IV's daughter, to Germany for her marriage to Lewis, Duke of Bavaria. As reward for this and other services he was granted custody and lordship of Bramber castle. He represented Sussex on four separate parliaments. He does not seem to have spent much time at Bodiam, for he placed the castle in trust with his sister Margaret and her husband, Thomas Sackville. When John died, without issue, the trustees surrendered the castle to his widow, Alice. It was later acquired, again by marriage, by Sir Thomas Lewknor in 1483, whose family held it for over 150 years.

Sir Thomas Lewknor was a Lancastrian and was attainted by Richard III. The king issued a commission, dated 8 November 1483, to the Earl of Surrey and other loyal nobles, authorising them 'to levy men in the counties of Kent and Sussex to besiege the castle of Bodyham which the rebels have seized'. The castle was apparently given up without a struggle for no damage was done to its walls at that time. Excavations have shown continuous habitation until the 17th century, so the theory that it became a ruin as a result of this siege is somewhat groundless. The Lewknors were re-established at Bodiam soon after the Battle of Bosworth Field in 1485.

From about the middle of the 16th century Bodiam passed to several of the minor heirs of the Lewknor family, the estate often being split up into smaller factions. John Tufton, 2nd Earl of Thanet, acquired the castle and entire estate between 1639–44, the period of the Civil War. Tufton was a staunch royalist, but in 1644 he sold Bodiam to Sir Nathaniel Powell, a parliamentarian. It is not known exactly when the castle was slighted, but it does not appear to have been actively involved in the war itself. It was certainly not bombarded nor subsequently dismantled by General Sir William Waller in 1643 as has been suggested—a theory which certain historians have continued to support. If it were true, the exterior walls would show signs of the bombardment, whereas the damage now visible is confined to the interior.

Its sale to a parliamentarian in 1644 may account for the slighting being relatively light. The exterior shell of walls and towers was left intact, and only the domestic buildings suffered damage. The castle was only inhabited again during a brief period in the late 18th century when a small cottage was erected against the internal face of the postern tower. The castle buildings suffered the usual fate of pilfering for their materials, but seem mostly to have been left to the gentle process of decay. When it was built the castle stood in a treeless landscape in the middle of extensive marshland. The marshes have been reclaimed and the scene softened by trees and green fields, which greatly add to the romance of the place. It was purchased by Marquess Curzon of Kedleston in 1916 and beautifully restored by him. He bequeathed it to the National Trust on his death in 1925.

The entrance front to Bodiam must present one of the finest facades of battlements and towers of any castle. The moat in which the castle stands is over three acres in extent and measures 542ft. by about 340ft. and is about eight feet deep. The castle sits on a levelled platform, some four feet above the water level, more-or-less in the middle of the lake. The walls revet this platform so as to rise sheer from the water and enclose an almost square area measuring, at its maximum distances, some 178ft. by 165ft. The walls are on average 6½ft. thick and rise 41ft. above the water, the towers rising a further twenty feet.

The castle is equipped with a large, circular drum tower at each corner and rectangular towers mid-way along the east and west walls. A third rectangular tower, designed as a postern, stands mid-way along the south side, while the north side is graced by the magnificent gate-house. It is a T-shaped structure with two rectangular towers, recessed back, flanking the entrance passage. Both the gatehouse and postern tower are heavily machicolated all round. Access can be made to the battlements of several of the towers, including the postern tower, giving the visitor a rare chance to inspect the machicolations at close quarters.

By the late 14th century the older style defences of medieval castles had passed from fashion. Gone were the great Norman keeps and

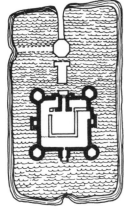

harbour

RIVER ROTHER
(to-day)

estuary edge
c. 1400 A.D.

encircling walls on castles built after that period, and in their place came the symmetrically-designed courtyard castles, such as Bodiam. They reverted to a much simpler plan and usually had great gatehouses to control the entrances. A new innovation was loop-holes in the walls for small guns. The gate passage was protected by *meutrieres*, machicolation-type openings in the roof of the passage; three portcullises, of which the lowermost part of the outer one survives in its raised position; and a drawbridge, with a second drawbridge in front of the barbican.

20. (*overleaf*) Aerial view showing the perfect symmetry of Bodiam Castle, along with its ruined interior, set within its lily-decked moat.

21. (*above*) Internal view of the gatehouse, Bodiam, from the battlements. Note the *meutrieres* in the vault of the entrance passage.

22. (*right*) These three arches (seen from the great hall) originally opened off from the screens passage and gave access to the buttery, pantry and kitchen at Bodiam.

23. A drawing of Bodiam Castle dated 1903, prior to restoration.

The lord's, garrison's and retainers' apartments which, as mentioned above, were kept separate from one another, were disposed around the four sides of the courtyard. The four drum towers at the corners were of hexagonal shape inside, and the south-west one contained a well.

Anyone seeking entry to the castle had to run a gauntlet of defences, continually exposed to fire from the defenders. The causeway crossing the moat to the octagon-shaped island is a modern addition. To reach the island, or barbican, one had to walk along a timber bridge connecting it to the bank from its west side, thus leaving an attacker completely exposed while crossing the moat. From the octagon a drawbridge protected the barbican, or outer gate, which in turn was separated from the gatehouse itself by a second drawbridge. Then, of course, the gatehouse with its many built-in defences had to be negotiated—a formidable task for even the bravest of aggressors.

Despite these quite sophisticated defences, however, there remains at Bodiam one serious weakness in its design. The moat is fed by natural springs, some of which rise in the bed of the moat itself and some a little way to the north-west of the castle. On the riverward side a sluice gate was inserted to maintain the water level, but easy access could be made to a high embankment in which it is situated. It would have been a comparatively simple task to have broken through this embankment near to the sluice and drain the moat, the whole time shielded from view of the castle and thus robbing it of its most effective single defence. At any rate, the castle was never put to arms, nor its weaknesses tested, and the moat has been drained only twice: by Lord Curzon, and in 1970 for dredging operations.

24. Remains of the chapel and Lady's Bower, seen from the battlements of Bodiam Castle.

The last word on Bodiam must rest with its chief benefactor, Lord Curzon, who so perfectly captured its atmospheric charm when he said of it:

> At Bodiam not only does the watery cincture remain, but no trace of the modern world appears to invade the ancient and solitary beauty of the scene, and it could hardly surprise anyone, were a train of richly clad knights, falcons on their wrists, and their ladies mounted on gaily caparisoned palfreys, suddenly to emerge from the Barbican Gate, for the enjoyment of the chase, or even were the flash of spearheads and the clatter of iron-shod hooves to indicate the exit of a party with more serious intent.

25. Viewed from the side, the surviving wall of the keep, Bramber Castle, looks like a giant monolith.

Bramber

(Brenbre. Brembre. Brambre. Old English bremer—broom thicket.)

The solitary monolith that remains of Bramber castle points its finger to the sky, apparently beckoning us to pause a while and listen to its tale. Its tale indeed is a doubly tragic one because of the ghastly fate of some of its past owners and because the castle walls have all but been demolished. What remains is a large knoll of land which looks artificial, but is, in fact, natural, with an artificial mound sitting more or less in the centre. The mound possibly dates from prehistoric times, later adapted for use as a castle motte by the Normans. One solitary fragment of the keep survives standing 76ft. high even in its ruination, a testament to its massive strength and the skill of its builders. To the right of the mound are the lower levels of some of the castle's domestic apartments, probably a kitchen and storerooms, preserving still some of their architectural details.

At first glance this would appear to be the extent of Bramber's remains, but outside the castle precincts, round the flattened circumference of the hill-top, a surprise awaits. Standing at about 10–12ft. high, and 15ft. in places, are the lower levels of the encircling curtain wall with about two-thirds of its length remaining. In places this wall can be seen inside the castle, too, amidst the brambles growing around the perimeter. The castle is built throughout of carefully knapped flints and pebbles, workmanship of a very high standard. It is interesting to note that some of the modern repair work itself now requires repair, whereas most of the original work beneath it does not. Mr. G. T. Clark, in *Medieval Military Architecture in England* (1884), best sums up Bramber's situation when he says:

> . . . in the construction of the fortress, advantage was taken of a knoll of the lower or grey chalk, roughly oval in figure and about 120ft. above the river. This was levelled on the top and scarped round the sides so as to form a more or less rounded area, 560ft. north and south, by 280ft. east and west. The scarp descended above 180ft. at an angle of 45ft. or a slope of one to one, into a ditch about 20ft wide at the bottom, and the opposite side of which, or counterscarp, rose about 40ft. at a similar angle, so that the ditch at the counterscarp level was 100ft. broad, and the crest of the scarp rose 30ft. to 40ft. above the ground opposite.

The artificial mound in its centre rose a further 40ft. so Bramber must once have been a most formidable fortress.

Soon after the Conquest William de Braose was granted the Rape and Honour of Bramber by the king, along with vast estates in Dorset, Hampshire and Wales. The family originated at a place called Brieuze, near Falaise in Normandy, from where they took their name, and the later Scottish royal family of Bruce was descended from them. They were a powerful family rising under the Norman kings to great position and wealth. Bramber castle became their principal seat in Sussex and passed through 15 of their family until it passed to the de Mowbrays, and was held by nine successive members of that family.

Thomas de Mowbray was created a Knight of the Garter for his distinguished military career, and in 1397 had the further honour of being created Duke of Norfolk. Three more Mowbrays were also created Knights of the Garter. The Honour and Rape of Bramber was afterwards conferred on the Howards, also Dukes of Norfolk, and so was eventually united with the neighbouring Rape of Arundel. The Howards chose not to live at Bramber, however, preferring their grander castle at Arundel. Bramber served for a while as a hunting-lodge, but afterwards fell into decay under the Seymours and later owners.

The singularly most notable, and at the same time most tragic, event there happened during the reign of King John, when the castle was owned by William de Braose. John feared the loss of de Braose's loyalty during the long and bitter struggles with his barons, so in 1208 he sent a messenger to Bramber castle demanding the custody of his children in return for his sworn allegiance. This story is retold under the entry for Knepp castle, but it is worth repeating here. Francis Grose, writing in the 18th century, so poignantly sums up the events that it is difficult not to feel saddened by the story, even after nearly 800 years:

> In the year 1208, King John suspecting divers of the nobility sent to demand hostages for their fidelity, among the rest to William de' Braose of whom his messengers demanded his children which Matilda his wife, according to Mathew Paris, gave this answer, that she could not trust her children with the King, who had so basely murdered his own nephew, Prince Arthur, whom he was in honour bound to protect. This speech being reported to the King, he was greatly incensed thereat and secretly sent soldiers to seize the whole family. But they receiving private information of his intent fled to Ireland, where he, in the year 1210, making them prisoners sent them to England and, closely confining them in Windsor Castle, he caused them to be starved to death. Some say William escaped to France where he shortly after died.

The ghosts of his two children are said to haunt the main street of Bramber each Christmas.

De Braose's estates were split up to some extent following this episode. Nearby Knepp castle was granted to John's son, the Duke of Cornwall, and became a great favourite of the king as a hunting retreat, but otherwise the castle descended along with that of Bramber. It was at this time that the de Mowbrays were installed at Bramber castle, following a brief occupation by King John himself between 1208–15 when he carried out extensive repairs.

It is not known when Bramber castle was finally deserted as a residence, but the mid–16th century seems likely. The castle was briefly occupied by parliamentary forces during the Civil War, first being taken by the royalists and then retaken by parliament under General Sir William Waller. Whilst it was in parliamentary hands King Charles is said to have passed through the village on his way to Brighton. The castle has since been torn down for its materials to construct roads in the area. It received this ruthless treatment at an apparently early date, because old engravings of the 18th century, by Hollar, show the castle very much as it is today. Its only distinction in later history was that it was one of the infamous 'rotten boroughs', regularly returning two members to parliament despite having, at times, as few as 18 voters. This was put right following the Reform Act of 1832.

The village of Bramber is quite delightful, full of interesting buildings, though it suffers from too much traffic. The church, alongside the castle, but on the side of the hill, is noteworthy, as is the 15th-century timber-framed house known as St Mary's. It contains in its basement the entrance to an underground passage, said to communicate with Bramber castle. Almost opposite the entrance to the castle, which is jointly administered by the National Trust and the Department of the Environment is an unique museum of pipes and smokiana.

26. A proposed, though slightly exaggerated, reconstruction of Bramber Castle, from an old drawing.

27. Aerial view showing the perfect symmetry of Camber Castle. The photo was taken prior restoration and the subsequent removal of the trees and bracken.

Camber

(Camere. Caumbre. Le Camber. From the French 'chambre' and Latin 'camera'—a room, confined space or harbour.)

When Henry VIII divorced Catherine of Aragon and set up the independent Church of England he incurred the full wrath of the Pope, who plotted with King Francis I of France and Emperor Charles V of Germany to invade England and re-establish papal authority. Only with their help could the Pope hope to succeed in his plans, so Henry sought to keep them at loggerheads. Henry had feared a French invasion for some time, and as early as 1520 had erected coastal fortifications in the West Country but, after 1538, when the Pope succeeded in reconciling the German and French leaders, the threat of a combined invasion became imminent.

In the short space of two years Henry built a chain of castles along the south, east and west coasts stretching from Hull to Cornwall. Not since the days of the Romans had a coastal defence scheme of such magnitude been undertaken. Although they are usually referred to as castles, technically they are really military forts or blockhouses, for defence by large cannons. However, though they were built primarily for coastal defence and were not a direct product of the feudal system, which had caused the great medieval castles to be built, they have stronger links with them than with the later artillery forts dating from the 17th to 19th centuries.

Henry built a proliferation of these castles in the South-East, most of them confined to Kent—such as Deal, Walmer, Sandown and Sandgate—but one was built in Sussex, at Camber, to protect Rye Haven. A circular tower already existed there, built between 1511-14, and Henry used this as the nucleus of his castle. Although the architects are not known for all of Henry's castles, the designer of Sandgate and Camber castles was Stephan von Haschenperg, a Bohemian—and Henry himself is believed to have had a hand in the designs.

In September 1486 Sir Richard Guldeford was granted lands near Rye, reclaimed from the sea, on condition that he built and maintained a tower there to defend Rye harbour. It is not known whether, in fact, he did build the tower, but in 1511 his son, Sir Edward, was given

£1,000 by the king to build a new tower at Camber, the name given to this area of marshland, which is probably the one existing when Henry VIII built his castle there in 1539. The original gun embrasures were blocked up and new, larger ones constructed. As originally built, this central tower was not unlike the Martello towers built nearly 300 years later along this same stretch of coast. It was but a short step in design from one to the other.

Camber castle is quite unlike any other of Henry's castles, and is second in size only to Deal; Deal Castle was 0.85 acre against Camber's 0.73 acre. It is octagonal in shape with four D-shaped bastions corresponding to the cardinal points of the compass at every alternate angle and a fifth, containing the entrance, at the north-west angle. It is perfectly symmetrical, as were most of Henry's other castles, though at close quarters the castle tends to lose something of its symmetry. It appears to be in a very battered condition for much of its facing stonework has been removed, but closer inspection reveals that it is almost untouched since its dismantling in 1642. Unlike other castles in Henry's chain, such as Deal and Walmer which were in use until comparatively recent times and were considerably altered as a result, Camber, even in its ruined state, remains much as Henry built it.

28. Camber Castle: looking through the entrance in the north-west bastion to the entrance of the central, circular tower. The loss of the outer facing stones has revealed the rubble and brick core of the walls.

Its walls, massively constructed of brick, but faced in a warm, sand-coloured stone, are 11ft. thick and stand to a height of about twenty feet. It would appear that its walls were never much higher than this, so it must always have had the same squat appearance. The central tower reaches a height of about 30ft. now and is 65ft. across. A string course traversing the building probably marks the height of the original tower. It is decorated with a series of ornate carvings, including the Tudor rose. The ashlar stonework of the whole castle is of a high standard, but here it is exceptionally fine. A curious and unique feature, though now much ruined, is a vaulted passageway around the external face of the central tower which communicated with four other passages, each leading to the D-shaped outer bastions. They connected with smaller, inverted D-shaped towers across the mouths of the outer bastions, in plan very much like two pairs of stirrups.

Recent excavations have shown that these smaller towers and passages are older than the outer bastions, but when those were built the stirrups remained in use as cavaliers. The ground level inside the castle is higher than outside, but was not always so. The vaulted passages of the stirrup bastions and around the base of the central tower partly remain, though they are now underground. Gun-loops in the walls of these passages indicate that originally they were above ground and intended to rake the courtyard with covering fire. Conditions inside the castle must have been cramped, for one of the flues from an oven in the kitchen, incorporated into one of the bastions, had to share a chimney with the smoke-vent of one of the gun embrasures.

A substantial section of the building accounts survive, though they refer mostly to Sandgate castle, but from them a fair assessment can be made of work carried out at Camber. Camber was begun in 1539 with a Mr. Molten as master mason—the most important and distinguished craftsman on a medieval building site. A Mr. Russell was appointed master carpenter, the second most important position. By April 1539, 1,272 workmen were engaged upon its construction, including bricklayers, stone layers, stonemasons, carpenters, hauliers, trench diggers, sawyers, and general labourers. Trees were felled in nearby Knell Wood to provide timber, while quarries at Hastings and Fairlight supplied the stone. It was customary for many of the bricks to be manufactured on site.

William Oxenbrigge was appointed paymaster and he became directly responsible for the castle's finances. He had to pay the workmen, purchase the necessary materials, and hire sub-contractors for specific tasks. He held the post until mid-1543 when he recorded the last payment in his accounts of £2,000 for the construction of a moat—or the 'water-works', as it is termed. Slight traces of the moat show today

on aerial photographs, but it was not normal for this type of fortress
to have a wet moat. More usual was a dry moat revetted in stone which
could be covered by cross-fire from the bastions, so references to
'water-works' may indicate some kind of plumbing installations and
water supply.

Finally, in July 1544 and at a total cost of £23,000, the castle
was completed (though it had probably been defensible some time
before that). Philip Chowte was installed at Camber as Captain, and
under his command were eight soldiers and six gunners—a comparatively
small force. By 1550 this was increased to 17 gunners and in 1584 a
further £170 was spent on the castle. Although the threat of invasion
from France passed, the castle was maintained for a further 50 years.

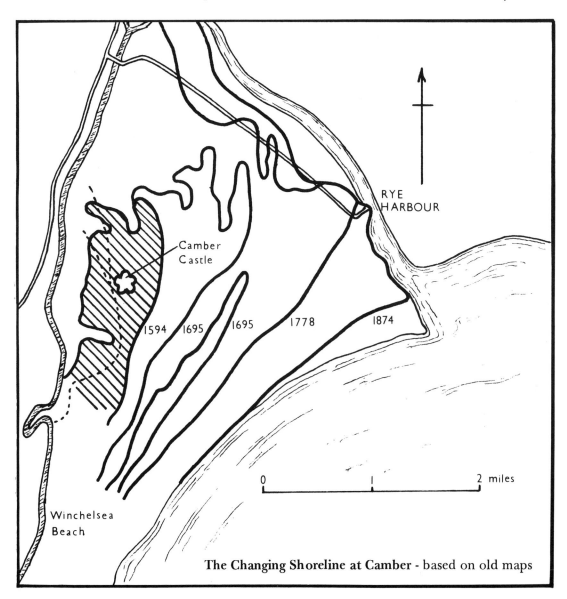

The Changing Shoreline at Camber - based on old maps

The real enemy of Camber proved not to be the ships of a foreign power, but the sea. After the violent storms of the 12th century the sea gradually began to recede, a process that was greatly accelerated in the 17th century. This, coupled with the silting-up of the river Rother, rendered the castle totally ineffective. When first built, Camber castle stood close to the water's edge, but by the mid-17th century it was separated from the sea by about a mile of shingle and marshland. Today the sea has retreated in places a further two miles. The sea, which for entirely opposite reasons had forced the inhabitants of Old Winchelsea to move their town to new ground, likewise sounded the death knell for Camber castle. It seems not to have played any part in the Civil War, for in August 1642 its guns were removed and transferred to Rye. The castle was ordered to be dismantled but, fortunately, this was not carried out too rigorously. Far more damage was done to its structure in later years when it was used as a convenient quarry for building materials.

Smuggling was rife throughout England from the 16th to 19th centuries and was considered a second occupation for many people. One of the centres of this illicit trade was the remote and lonely marshland of Kent and Sussex. A gang of smugglers used Camber castle as their base, storing their contraband in the vaulted passages and chambers of the old fortress. On one occasion in the 19th century a fierce battle broke out between the smugglers and the revenue men— apparently, that was the only time Camber castle has ever witnessed a fight of any kind throughout its history!

Apart from the roofs, floors and fittings (long since removed), the shell of the castle remains complete today and is undergoing restoration by the Department of the Environment. It is soon to be opened to the public—though the exterior can be viewed from a public footpath. In the meantime, the fort slumbers on undisturbed, with only sheep for company against the solitude of the vast Romney Marsh. I was fortunate enough to witness two working sheep dogs in action when I visited, which somehow added to the incongruity of this lonely castle now standing in lush meadows—a far cry from the picture this stretch of coast must have presented in Henry VIII's day.

29. Chichester Castle: the sad, mutilated remains of the castle mound, with the priory church of the Grey Friars beyond.

Chichester

(Cisseceastre. Ciceastre. Cheechester. Cissa's ceaster.)

The account that follows should perhaps more appropriately be included in the 'Lost Castles' section of this book, for Chichester castle has long been razed to the ground. However, its history is important and interesting enough to warrant its inclusion here. When, soon after the Conquest, the lands of Sussex were divided into six Rapes, each held with a strong castle, Chichester was included among them. Its castle soon may have been demolished, but the Rape of Chichester, and all the military and administrative paraphernalia that that entailed, remained throughout the Middle Ages, much of the land being held by the bishops of this cathedral city.

The town of Chichester had long been considered important and the Romans protected it with a mighty wall. They knew the place as Noviomagus (not Regnum as is often stated) and their wall survives as the core of the present medieval city walls. The walls were first erected around A.D. 200 and received massive bastions for additional strength about 50 years later. Long lengths of this wall survive today in good condition, forming an almost complete circuit. During the 18th century an earthen rampart was thrown up against the inner face of the wall to provide a promenade and it still forms a very attractive walk.

Soon after the Conquest a motte and bailey castle was erected within the city walls. The mound survives, but shows no signs of a stone keep ever having been constructed on its summit. The city wall itself was used to form part of the castle defences, which were further protected by the erection of a wall across the north-east corner of the city to form a large single bailey. The castle was most probably built by Roger de Montgomery, although the name Earl d'Alencon also appears in early records. It stood on the site now occupied by Priory Park and appears to have been a fairly important stronghold for by 1142 it already had a large chapel and repairs were made to its defences in 1176.

The main event of importance attaching to the castle occurred in 1193 when John attempted to seize the crown of England during Richard I's imprisonment abroad whilst on crusade. Records show us that the castle was provisioned with sufficient stores to withstand a

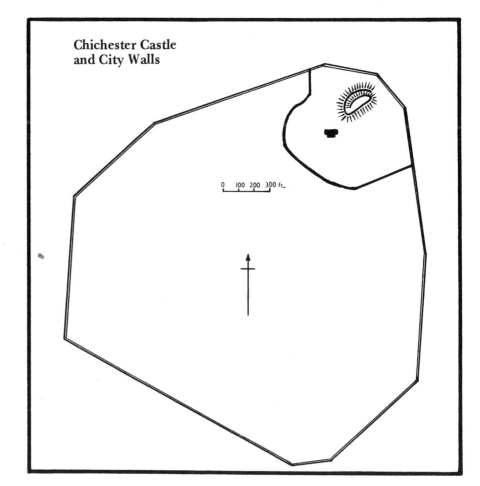

Chichester Castle
and City Walls

0   100 200 300 ft.

long siege, including plentiful supplies of bacon, barley, beans and
ammunition. In the following year five knights were brought in to
help garrison the castle. They remained there for only 24 days, but a
tantalising gap in the records prevents us from learning whether John's
forces ever actually attacked the castle. Certainly in both 1194 and
1195 there are entries in the accounts for the purchase of materials
for repairs to the houses and chapel within the castle. (The various
outbuildings within castle baileys were referred to in the Middle Ages
as the 'houses within the castle.')

In 1198 the castle was used as a gaol and placed in the charge of
William Marshall, Earl of Pembroke and Sheriff of Sussex. He was
succeeded as Constable in 1208 by Richard de Mucegras. In 1215
instructions were given by Matthew FitzHerbert, then Sheriff, to the

citizens of Chichester to strengthen the city defences, but they appear to have excluded the castle itself. The following year King John ordered its destruction in case it should fall into the hands of the invading Prince Louis, Dauphin of France, who had been invited by some of the barons to take the English crown. The castle was not destroyed, and John's anxieties were later justified when Louis successfully attacked and captured the castle. It was retaken early in 1217 and an entry in the Patent Rolls for that year decreed that the castle should be 'thrown down and destroyed to its foundations'. The destruction was carried out by Philip d'Albini and was so complete that nothing remains today except the grassy mound. In the Civil War the mound is believed to have been used in 1642 as a battery during the Siege of Chichester and was much mutilated as a result.

The castle site was given by Richard, Earl of Cornwall, to the Order of the Grey Friars in 1269. They erected a priory there using the castle stone in their buildings. Part of the castle chapel may have been incorporated into the priory church, which still stands, and the castle gatehouse may have been retained as the entrance to the priory; the ruined gatehouse near the church shows some signs of having once been a defensible building.

When the Order of the Grey Friars was dissolved in 1538 the site was afterwards given to the people of Chichester. They converted the chancel into a guildhall and leased the remaining land to a John Knott in 1543. He built a large house there adjoining the church, which afterwards passed through many distinguished families' hands before being acquired, in 1824, by the Duke of Richmond. In 1918 the 7th Duke presented the site to the city for use as a public recreation ground (for which use it had been held in trust since 1851).

It is still used as a park today and gives no hint of the medieval castle that once stood on the green and pleasant lawns. The mound is greatly reduced in height and stands adjacent to a children's playground. A park seat has been placed on its summit for those who wish to rest a while and ponder on the historic events enacted on this site some seven centuries before. The sad story of this castle bears a marked similarity to that of Canterbury castle, Kent's counterpart cathedral city.

30. A restored section of the city wall, Chichester, and one of the gateways, showing the earthen rampart erected in the 18th century.

31. The fire-charred remains of the entrance front, Cowdray Castle. Note the gun loops in the gatehouse. Despite its ruined appearance, one can still imagine how spectacular it must once have been.

Cowdray

(Codray. From old French coudraie—a hazel hedge.)

The majestic remains of Cowdray castle stand at the end of a public footpath from a car park in the centre of Midhurst. The footpath crosses the water meadows of the river Rother—a tributary of the Arun. The castle owes its present location to the de Bohuns, the earliest recorded owners. The original castle at Midhurst stood on the summit of St Anne's Hill on the opposite side of the river, but in 1273 John de Bohun decided to rebuild his castle on a new site. Where the present Cowdray castle now stands, he erected a moated castle of some size, traces of which were found during repair work.

The story of Cowdray is a tragic one, to which the fire-charred ruins bear witness. When the last of the Bohuns died in 1492 Cowdray passed to a son-in-law, Sir David Owen. Instead of up-dating the castle, he decided completely to rebuild it in the new Tudor fashion. What he built is really not a castle at all, but a large semi-fortified mansion. However, the principles of medieval fortification were still very much in architects' minds, and although Cowdray could not have resisted a full-scale siege it was certainly strong enough to withstand a considerable onslaught.

It represents one of the finest, and earliest, examples of a transitional building erected at a time when castles proper of the Middle Ages were fresh enough in people's minds to be remembered, yet when the gentry were beginning to move out from behind the protection and confinement of their castle walls in preference for more graciously designed houses. Later houses were built either with no defences at all or at most with mock defences only, such features as battlements being added as architectural embellishments, but Cowdray was actually capable of offering a stout, if not a prolonged, resistance.

The house built by Sir David Owen was arranged around a central courtyard, measuring some 125ft. by 100ft. Much of the present ruin dates from this time, including the eastern and northern ranges, the great hall, the chapel with its three-sided apse, and the unusual hexagonal-shaped kitchen tower, which is still complete. Although Sir David continued to live there until his death in 1535, he had, in

55

32. Cowdray Castle, showing the kitchen tower to the left and the ruined chapel, right, with its three-sided apse.

fact, sold it to Sir William Fitzwilliam in 1529. Fitzwilliam was a great favourite of the king and was created Earl of Southampton in 1537, and, two years later, Lord Keeper of the Privy Seal. In 1533 he had obtained a licence to crenellate his house at Cowdray, but seems not to have acted upon it until after 1535 when Sir David Owen died.

Most of the rest of the house was built by Fitzwilliam, including the impressive gatehouse with its twin turrets to front and rear, and it remains virtually unaltered to this day. The core of the house is built from brick, but it is almost entirely encased in a beautiful cream-coloured stone. Most of the defences, such as they are, are contained within the gatehouse and entrance range, which were provisioned with gun-loops and battlements. For the rest, the house is largely undefended and presents a spectacle of large, mullioned windows of the Perpendicular style. Numerous engravings were made both of the interior and exterior prior to its destruction by fire in the late 18th century, revealing a magnificently appointed house with fine furnishings. The great hall, which had a beautiful hammer-beam roof, has been likened to Hampton Court Palace and the grand staircase was painted by the celebrated artist Pellegrini between 1708–13. In overall appearance it is not unlike Shurland Hall, a structure of similar date on the Isle of Sheppey, in Kent.

From Sir William Fitzwilliam Cowdray passed to his half-brother, Sir Anthony Browne, another favourite of the king. Henry VIII conferred Battle abbey and its estates upon Sir Anthony, and he is reported to have turned the monks out of their home and converted the abbey into a comfortable house for his own use. There is a story connected with this of how the last monk to leave the abbey laid a curse on Sir Anthony, saying that the last of his family would perish by fire and water. The curse took on a grim reality some years later when not only did the family line die out, but Cowdray castle was destroyed by fire, thus reducing it to its present condition.

Sir Anthony Browne had been made Viscount Montague in 1554 (his coat of arms can be seen in a panel on the gatehouse) and Cowdray remained in his family's hands until the tragic year of 1793. On 25 September, workmen employed repairing the south wing carelessly left a charcoal pan burning which toppled over and set fire to the house. The splendid and priceless collection of furniture, tapestries and paintings was destroyed and most of the house was completely gutted. Ironically, the Kitchen Tower, normally the part of a house carrying the highest fire risk, was the only part not damaged by the flames.

Eight days later the last of the family line, the 8th Viscount Montague, was drowned while attempting to shoot the rapids of Laufenburg on the river Rhine. As if to add a final, sinister touch to the story, in 1815 the two sons of the then owners, the Poyntz family,

33. Cowdray Castle: part of the ruined entrance front with its gracious mullioned windows. The kitchen tower beyond is unusual in being hexagonal-shaped, with ingeniously designed chimneys in the corner buttresses.

34. An old print of Cowdray Castle showing the entrance front prior to its destruction by fire in 1793.

were drowned at Bognor Regis. The Poyntzs had been living in the Keeper's Lodge on the estate, but after this disaster that, too, was deserted. And so Cowdray remained, a gaunt, half-forgotten, ivy-clad ruin until its purchase in 1908 by Sir Weetman Dickinson Pearson, created Viscount Cowdray in 1916. He enlisted the services of Sir William St John Hope to preserve the ruins and compile a history of the castle.

Cowdray has always been much frequented by royalty. In 1538 it was visited by Henry VIII, and in 1552 Edward VI paid a call. In his journal he remarked of Cowdray: 'the goodly house of Sir Anthony Browne's, where we were marvelously, yea rather excessively banketted'. In 1591 Elizabeth I stayed at the house for a whole week; she habitually dropped in on her subjects at a moment's notice and stayed for extended periods, while the poor hosts were often at their wits end trying to please her and competing with one another for her favours. Sir Anthony spared no expense and entertained her in considerable luxury. She is reputed to have shot a deer while in Sussex—perhaps in the 600-acre Cowdray Park.

Sir Anthony Browne's close relationship with Elizabeth is all the more intriguing because while the monarch was of the new faith—a Protestant—he was unashamedly a devout Catholic. He was, however, totally loyal to the crown and during the perilous times of the Spanish Armada he, with his son and grandson, led a large army to the camp at Tilbury to meet the Spanish threat.

During the Civil War the Brownes held Cowdray for the king, but on the approach of Waller's troops in December 1643 they abandoned the castle. The parliamentarians looted the place, taking a great many valuables and stripping it of many of its fine fittings. An order was issued for the castle to be slighted, but this was never carried out for fear of upsetting the locals who were staunch royalists and Catholics. Instead, William Cawley was placed there with a small garrison. After the death of Richard Cromwell in 1659 Colonel Fagge took up residence, but after the Restoration it was returned to the Montagues. It remained with them until the tragedy of 1793.

The present Cowdray House is largely a Victorian mansion, built on the opposite side of the park to the castle. Both the house and park are frequently visited by royalty, because Cowdray is a premier centre for polo tournaments in this country, often playing host to such familiar royal figures as Prince Philip and Prince Charles.

35. The well-tended and highly picturesq
ruins of Crowhurst Castle are well cared fc
by the present owner, in whose garden the
stand.

Crowhurst

(Croherste. Crauherste. Crowhurst. Crow-frequented wooded hill.)

The scant remains of Crowhurst castle stand romantically preserved as part of a private garden in the village of Crowhurst. Never really a castle proper, rather it was a fortified manor house and, while never the object of any siege, it has played a significant part in Sussex history.

The manor of Crowhurst first appears in 772 when Offa gave eight hides of land there to Oswald, Bishop of Selsey. Later it came into the possession of Earl Harold, but following his defeat at Hastings the manor was granted by the Conqueror to the Count of Eu as part of the Rape of Hastings. The count never resided at Crowhurst, however, which was sub-let to various tenants under the castle guard system. In 1086 we find it in the possession of Walter Fitzlambert, who is believed to have rebuilt it after its devastation by the Normans soon after the Battle of Hastings. A later descendant of his was Walter de Scotney who inherited the manor and, in the reign of Richard I, gave the church at Crowhurst to Hastings Priory.

Walter's son, Peter de Scotney, became Standard Bearer to the Count of Eu and performed castle guard service at Hastings castle. His son, another Walter, was chief Steward to Richard, Earl of Gloucester, and it is from his time, about 1250, that most of the present remains date. However, he was the last of the Scotneys to live at Crowhurst, for in 1259 he was executed for attempting to poison the Earl of Gloucester and his half-brother William de Clare. All his estates were confiscated by Henry III and later granted to Prince Edward. It seems that, after Walter de Scotney's attempt to poison his master, his manor at Crowhurst was ransacked by Edward and made uninhabitable, in which sorry state it remained for about a hundred years.

The manor and lands of Crowhurst continued through successive tenants until, while in the hands of the Dukes of Brittany, it appears to have been separated from the rest of the Rape of Hastings and held directly from the king. Between 1358–60 Crowhurst underwent repairs at the hand of John, Earl of Richmond, and it seems most likely that it was then that the manor-house received its fortifications.

These were probably never very substantial, and all trace of them has gone today.

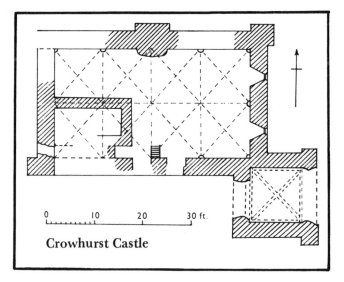

0   10   20   30 ft.

Crowhurst Castle

This small manor continued to play an important part in the power struggles of the later Middle Ages and included among its beneficiaries were Sir Edward Dalyngrigge, Sir John Devereux, and Ralph, Earl of Westmorland. When the earl died in 1412 Henry IV granted it to Sir John Pelham. The history of Crowhurst then becomes confused, for in 1445 the Rape of Hastings was acquired by Sir Thomas Hoo, and both he and his successor, William Lord Hastings, laid claim to the manor as still part of the Rape. In 1465, however, the then owner, Sir John Pelham, was acknowledged as the rightful heir to Crowhurst, which then continued to be held in demesne. It remained in Pelham hands until 1838 when it passed, by marriage, to the Papillons.

The house became ruined during the Pelham ownership when, in the early 17th century, a new house was begun in Crowhurst Park. Although the ruins are sparse the quality of the stone used and the elegance of design speak of a once fine residence of noble proportions. A certain amount of confusion has arisen in descriptive accounts of the castle about what the present remains represent, at various times described as both a hall and a chapel. However, I believe the ruins represent the north range of a once substantial group of buildings and are neither hall nor chapel. At the south-east corner of the main building are the ruins of a two-storeyed porch, which I believe once gave access to a hall, now vanished, but which stretched away to the south. The porch probably gave access to the screens passage.

The more substantial of the two surviving rooms may well have been a chapel, as has been suggested, but its size (40ft. by 22ft.) would render that unlikely. Considering the stately proportions of the rest of the manor and the importance of its various owners, it seems more likely that it formed part of a grand suite of apartments for the use of the lord. Perhaps further excavations at the site will reveal more about its layout (although on private property the ruins are inspected periodically by the Department of the Environment). The present owner takes a great deal of pride in this small piece of England's heritage entrusted to his care, and chatted to me most enthusiastically about it.

Both the main building and the porch were vaulted throughout and while the vaults themselves have long since collapsed, corbels remain on the walls from where they sprang and portions of the supporting ribs are to be seen on the ground. The east end-wall of the main room is the better preserved and stands almost to its full height of about 30ft. At ground floor level are two lancet-type windows, while above them are the remains of a large and splendid window of the Decorated period. Most of the other walls are reduced to foundation level or lower courses only.

This small, though interesting, castle retains a certain charm, a feeling enhanced by its picturesque location immediately next to the church. A fine view of it can be had from the churchyard.

36. This view of Crowhurst Castle shows two lancet windows with a large window of the Decorated style above, perhaps the remains of a chapel.

37. Ruins of the collegiate church, Hastings Castle, with one of the early Norman towers beyond.

Hastings

(Haestingaceaster. Haestinga. Hasting. Haesten's ceaster.)

Sussex possesses castles representative of most basic types to be found
in this country. Arundel has a central mound with two baileys; Lewes
has two mounds, one on either side of a central bailey area; Fulking is a
fine example of a motte and bailey reduced to earthworks only;
Pevensey possesses a Norman tower keep set within the walls of a
Roman fort; Bodiam, seeming to float on its lily-decked moat, is a
perfect example of a courtyard castle, and Herstmonceux is an impressive brick-built, castellated mansion. The list goes on. At Hastings we
have a type of fortress known as a promontory or cliff-top castle, to
complete this magnificent collection of castles. A promontory fortress
was achieved by constructing a wall and ditch across the neck of an
otherwise inaccessible part of a cliff-top.

The visitor to Hastings castle today must leave the site slightly
disappointed. The very name 'Hastings' conjures up in everyone's
mind all manner of romantic images. One expects to see a castle here
of considerable size. I have visited the castle often and have overheard
the frequent remark that, were it not for the magnificent view, the
trip to the cliff-top would scarcely have been worthwhile. Such
judgement is a little harsh, but only a fraction of this once considerable
castle remains. Erosion and the deliberate demolition of part of the
cliff face to provide more room for the town below have destroyed
much of the castle, making it difficult to visualise the place as it once
was. For this reason I include a plan here. Readers might be surprised
to learn of the castle's original extent, both to the east along the
cliff-top and southwards out into the sea.

Hastings castle, notwithstanding the loss of its greater part, still has
much of interest within its walls. There are two ways to the castle site.
One, the more leisurely, is to take the cable railway from the promenade
through a tunnel cut into the cliffs. The second, not to be recommended
unless you are fit, is to clamber up the cliff face. Although the cliffs
here are about 200ft. high they are sandstone and relatively easy to
climb, as the rock provides many footholds. If you have a head for
heights and are sure-footed, then this is the more pleasurable method.

38. A very unusual aerial view showing the magnificent cliff-top setting of Hastings Castle. The ruins show up well, as does the enormous ditch cut through the rock to form this promontory fortress.

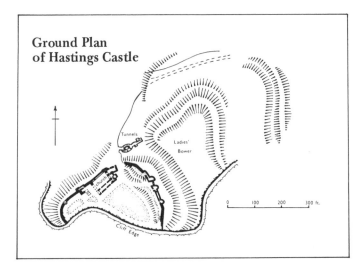

Ground Plan
of Hastings Castle

Tunnels

Ladies'
Bower

Church

Cliff Edge

0   100   200   300 ft.

Here would be a good point to relate the events leading up to 1066. For many years the reason stated for Duke William of Normandy's claim to the English throne was that he had, the previous year, imprisoned Harold Godwin, heir to the English throne who, in order to secure his freedom, had promised to relinquish his rights to the throne in favour of Duke William. The real reasons, however, behind William's claim are much more complex. Some historians believe he had a blood-tie with Edward the Confessor, then king, and actually had a stronger claim to the throne than Harold. Others maintain that his claim was merely a pretext to give him an excuse to invade England. Whatever the truth, Duke William of Normandy did contest Harold's right to the throne in 1066 and plotted with Hardrada, King of Norway, to take the crown by force.

Throughout summer 1066 Harold had been guarding the south coast of England with both an army and a fleet of ships. He knew Duke William and his invading force waited in readiness on the other side of the Channel for the strong winds, then prevalent, to change in his favour. William bided his time, inducing in the English a false sense of security. On 8 September Harold considered the position safe enough to allow the bulk of his army, which was mostly made up from the local fyrd, to return to their fields and bring in the harvest. Harold returned to London where he received news that the combined armies of Hardrada and Tostig, his half-brother, had landed in Yorkshire. Defence of the north had been entrusted to the earls Edwin and Morcar, but they were beaten at Fulford. Harold was forced to march to Yorkshire with his army, calling up local fyrds on the way. He met the invading army on 25 September at Stamford Bridge, where he utterly defeated them.

The invasion by Hardrada and Tostig, as Harold afterwards discovered to his peril, was but one arm of a well-planned pincer movement. While Harold was otherwise engaged in the north, Duke William sailed unopposed across the Channel to Pevensey where he had time to set up camp and ferry across all the troops and equipment he needed for his conquest. Harold received news of the landing and was forced to march his already weary army all the way back to the south coast. Many of the untrained soldiers are reported to have left his cause on the way, facing him with the problem of calling up sufficient men from fyrds in the south. On 14 October the two armies finally met, the result of which is well known.

The Bayeux tapestry records the story of William's rise to fame, and his invasion of England. One of the scenes shows workmen erecting a 'ceastra', or castle at Hesteng (Hastings). The Normans are known to have brought prefabricated wooden panels across with them to

construct a timber motte and bailey castle on their arrival, thought
to be the one erected at Hastings. The mound of this first castle can
still be seen on the cliff-top site. It has been said that no fortress of
any kind had stood on the cliffs at Hastings prior to the erection of
the Norman castle, but the mound may well be of prehistoric date,
later adapted by the Normans. A little further along the cliffs can be
seen the earthworks of a fortified camp, possibly Roman. The Danes
may also have built a fortress here under Haesten.

Once the castle had been established it rapidly developed into a
building of some size—covering an area of 11 acres—and importance.
Hastings was an original member of the Cinque Ports and once
possessed a good harbour. In the 11th century the cliff on which the
castle stands extended much further into the sea, and the sea itself
lapped the shore much closer inland, thus creating a perfect natural
haven protected at its mouth by the castle. Violent storms of the
13th and later centuries were to change all that, for the sea has since
receded and the cliffs have suffered much erosion and the deliberate
removal of parts of them to create a promenade in fashionable
19th-century Hastings. The castle, as it appeared in the 12th century,
however, must have been a formidable sight, perched high on its
cliff-top setting.

After landing at Pevensey, the Conqueror sent his half-brother, Odo,
Bishop of Bayeux, to Hastings where he erected the motte and bailey
castle referred to above. After his victory Duke William set about
the division of Sussex into six Rapes, of which Hastings formed the
easternmost and, for a time, the most important. The castle was granted
first to Humphrey de Tilliol, Hugh de Grantmaisnil's brother-in-law,
who returned to Normandy in 1070. Robert, Count of Eu, the
Conqueror's uncle, was then granted the entire Rape of Hastings.

39. Hastings Castle: the truncated
stump of one of the gatehouse
towers, with a 13th-century drum
tower beyond.

It is to this powerful Norman lord that we probably owe the very early replacement in stone of the castle's timber defences. He also established a collegiate church within the castle, which remained in use until the reign of Henry VIII, long after the castle ceased to be of importance. He established there a dean and eight canons who, although housed within the castle precincts, remained separate from it. Thomas Becket was at one time dean of the church, and his troubled spirit is still reputed to haunt the site. The rest of the castle dates mainly from the 12th and 13th centuries, and Henry II was responsible for much of the work. In 1172 we find reference to the erection of a keep, or great tower, but it is not certain whether this was a shell keep on the summit of the mound, or a separate tower in that part of the castle now lost to the sea.

The Counts of Eu retained possession of the castle for five generations, except for frequent interludes when it was occupied by the king. William Rufus seized it on one occasion, as did Henry II and King John, of whom the latter also ordered its destruction in 1216 for fear of its falling into French hands. The castle was subsequently 'slighted', but later repaired by Henry III. Alice, Countess of Eu, succeeded to the estate and on her marriage to Ralph de Ysenden it passed into his family. His son, William de Ysenden, lost it again to Henry III by escheat and it was then granted to Prince Edward for a time. It reverted to Henry III, who granted the Honour and Rape of Hastings to Peter of Savoy, Earl of Richmond, in 1254 in exchange for property in Norfolk, but the king held on to the castle for his own use. Savoy's grandson, John Rufus, succeeded to the Honour and Rape in 1269, but the castle was still excluded from the inheritance and remained in royal hands, passing next to Edward I. Hastings was still a major port of embarkation to the Continent, so we can understand the crown's eagerness to secure the castle.

Hastings castle was never attacked by a military force, as far as is known, but it was frequently the scene of minor attacks by the local population on the church within its walls. As so often in the Middle Ages the bitter conflicts between church and state, and church and people, were often more damaging than an invading army from France might have been.

In 1331, while the castle was still in the hands of the crown in the person of Edward III, the defences were found to be lacking. The sea had caused considerable damage to the castle, so much so that the dean complained to the king. Apparently, there were gaps in the walls and the church buildings were in a dilapidated state, allowing people from the town to help themselves to the church's treasures. Since the castle was no longer of any real military importance,

Edward III gave custody of the castle to the dean and chapter, allowing them to put it into repair on condition that they surrender it to the crown in time of war. In 1339 French ships sailed into Hastings harbour and plundered both the town and castle. Fearing that a similar attack might follow, Edward sent the Earl of Surrey to protect the coast, and installed William de Percy in the castle as Warden.

The joint custodianship of church and state, however, could not have been expected to last long without conflict. De Percy took his duties as Warden too seriously, operating the castle as a garrison and refusing the clergy and visiting pilgrims free access to their church and buildings, which had assumed the proportions of a small monastery. The dean complained to the king who ordered de Percy not to interfere with the daily life of the church.

The trouble did not end with the resolution of this dispute, for in 1343 and again in 1366 there were problems of a different kind. The clergy, in their cliff-top castle, were not popular with the townspeople below who attacked the castle at night, scaling the walls with ladders and robbing the church of its valuables. Trouble of this nature continued at the castle until its abolition by order of Henry VIII.

The castle was granted to various overlords, despite its obsolescence, until it was purchased by Sir William, later Lord Hastings, in the 15th century. Sir William was a distant descendant of the Eu family, so the castle ownership had come full circle. It was purchased by Sir Thomas Pelham in 1591 for £2,500 and remained in that family until 1951, when it was bought by Hastings Corporation and opened to the public as a park.

What remains today is about half of the inner bailey. The earthworks of the middle bailey, the 'Ladies Bower', can still be traced on the cliff-top at the other side of the castle ditch, which separated the two enclosures. Faint traces of a third, outer bailey are just visible beyond that. It is not certain, however, if these two additional baileys were ever considered important enough to be consolidated in stone.

The remains, though scanty, are not without interest. They consist principally of the ruins of the collegiate church of St Mary, of which the chancel arch and nave are the most substantial portions. Immediately beyond is a small square tower of early date, projecting internally rather than externally from the wall face. To the east of the church is the mound, and beyond that the stump of the gatehouse, which consisted of two roughly D-shaped towers. Most of the curtain wall survives in an arc between the two cliff edges, in places nearly 20ft. high. Part of the wall south of the gatehouse, where it connects with a fourth tower, preserves a galleried passage within its thickness which would originally have provided a two-tier wall-walk to the curtain.

40. From a print dated 1860 showing Hastings Castle ruins as a fashionable picnic spot.

The ditch, cut from the rock and very deep, is about 100ft. wide in places.

One last, visible feature at Hastings castle is a curious series of galleries cut into the rock beneath the mound. They are called 'the only whispering dungeons in Great Britain' in the castle's publicity literature, and consist of two arched passageways, the longer one about 45ft. in length, each ending in a small chamber. They were described in 1877 by the Rev. E. Marshall as dungeons, a tradition which persists today. An excellent, enthusiastic guide tells modern visitors how poor wretches were incarcerated there and secrets extracted, pointing to slight pock-marks and indentations in the walls, indicating manacles and the rubbing of prisoners' heads. There is, however, absolutely no factual basis for this, even though the story adds colour to the castle's history. Much more research is needed on such subterranean works before final judgements can be made. They may have existed in a pre-Conquest, pre-fortified mound.

41. The mound, Hastings Castle, crowned by what may be the remains of a shell keep. The archway to the left gives access to the underground passages.

If the remains of Hastings castle are a disappointment, their story is still fascinating, and the magnificent site deserves to be visited. The view from the castle ramparts is both breathtaking and exhilarating, a marvellous panorama of the town and countryside below.

Herstmonceux Castle: the romantic
and highly picturesque entrance front,
seen across the lake.

Herstmonceux

(From Herst, or Hurst—a wood, and 'Monceux', family name of its one-time owners. Hence, Herst-Monceux.)

The pristine beauty of Herstmonceux castle, seen across the wide expanse of its moat, is unforgettable. It was built unusually in brick, at a time when castles were already out of date, but when nobles still clung tenaciously to the prestige of living in a castle. Unlike the 'sham' castles of later centuries, however, Herstmonceux, with its 4ft.-thick walls, was capable of offering resistance if attacked. The impressive gatehouse, with a drawbridge, double parapet and continous row of machicolations, was built not merely as a decorative architectural feature, but was equipped with gun and arrow loops. Some critics have harshly described Herstmonceux as an elaborate folly, not designed for serious defence. Though it could not have withstood a prolonged siege, it would be fair to call it a fortified manor house.

The castle was built in 1440 and by 1777 it had been dismantled; an active life of just 300 years. The manor itself, however, is considerably older, and in the time of Edward the Confessor was held by Edmer, a priest. After the Conquest it became part of the Rape of Hastings and by the Domesday Survey it formed part of the Count of Eu's estates. It was then known simply as Herst, but a century later the Norman family of de Monceux came into possession of it, and suffixed their name to distinguish it from other 'Hursts' in the south of England. No castle existed then but a fine manor house stood on the site, the owners of which had to pay castle service to Hastings castle.

William de Monceux became Constable of Pevensey castle; on his death in 1243 custody of his estates was given to Bernard of Savoy until his son, Waleron, came of age. Waleron de Monceux played a significant part in the barons' wars, siding with Simon de Montfort. His lands appear not to have been confiscated by the king as a result of his involvement in the rebellion, for on his death, in about 1296, they passed to his son, John. The next two successors to the estate were also named John, of whom the latter succeeded in 1316, after which the family line of de Monceux died out. By 1331 the manor had passed to John de Fiennes by his marriage to John de Monceux's sister, Maud. He was succeeded in 1351 by his son, William, but, when he died in 1359, some years before his wife, she was granted one-third of the manor in bower while the rest was held by Queen Philippe in custody until the rightful heir came of age.

When John de Fiennes, the heir in question, came of age he held the entire manor, but he, too, died prematurely in 1375 leaving no son, so the manor passed to his brother William, also a minor. Herstmonceux was held in custody of the king until William came of age, and when he died in 1403, at the age of only 46, the estate passed to his son Roger. Roger de Fiennes became a soldier of some repute and it is under him that Herstmonceux saw its most active and profitable years, for he was the builder of the present castle.

Sir Roger played a prominent role in the French wars, afterwards known as the Hundred Years' War, and accompanied Henry V many times in battle, including at Agincourt. He acquired great wealth, taken from the spoils of war, and amassed a huge personal fortune. He became Treasurer of the Household to Henry VI, and in 1430 Sir John Pelham released him from all-commitment to the Honour of Hastings. Herstmonceux thus became an independent manor no longer responsible for castle guard or any other services to Hastings castle, and soon became very important in its own right. The existing humble manor house was no longer considered an appropriate residence for so important a person as Sir Roger, so he sought permission from the king to build himself a castle. He received a royal licence in 1440 to crenellate his house, but instead chose to demolish his old manor house and rebuild it completely.

The site chosen for his new castle was on low ground close to a stream, used to feed the moat via a series of small lakes. The castle took the form of a large square, some 214ft. by 206ft. externally, arranged around a series of four courtyards, and was built almost entirely from brick, stone being used only as door and window dressings. Because the bricks used are a little over nine inches in length, slightly longer than the usual English brick, it has perhaps wrongly been assumed that the designer and builders of the castle were of Flemish birth. There is, however, no reason to suppose that the builders were not English, but working perhaps under the guidance of a Flemish master.

The outstanding feature and focal point of the castle is the splendid gatehouse. It is a lofty structure some 85ft. high, and consists of two octagonal towers of slender proportions which change, above a corbelled string course, to a circular shape. This is then crowned with a battlemented and heavily machicolated parapet. Rising above this

43. An unusual view of the gatehouse, Herstmonceux Castle, showing the parapet and machicolations.

level are two further circular turrets of smaller diameter, thus giving two tiers of battlements. It is this striking feature of the gatehouse that renders it so singularly attractive. The rest of the castle exterior, which is in immaculate condition and almost entirely original, consists of a high enclosing wall containing two storeys of apartments, with a

44. The entrance front of Herstmonceux showing the magnificent double-parapeted gatehouse.

number of fine windows much in evidence. There are projecting octagonal-shaped towers at each corner, rising above the level of the wall-top, and three intermediate towers along each face, generally rising only to second-storey level. The centre tower of the north face has been enlarged to contain a smaller, rear gatehouse, and the south face contains four intermediate towers, the two larger, central ones forming the main gatehouse. Internally the castle consisted of a series of interconnecting rooms arranged around the four courtyards, but these were dismantled in 1777, the present interior being a modern replacement. Drawings made before their demolition reveal the original apartments to have been most stately, and the great hall was comparable to those still to be seen in the colleges of Oxford and Cambridge.

Sir Roger could scarcely have lived long enough to appreciate the full beauty of his castle, for he died in 1449, leaving it to his son Richard. He married Joan, daughter and heiress of Thomas Lord Dacre, and consequently adopted the family name of Dacre in preference to Fiennes presumably to assist his social advancement. Richard became Sheriff of Sussex and Surrey in 1452 and Chamberlain to Edward IV's queen. Herstmonceux passed to his grandson, Thomas, on his death, his eldest son John having predeceased him. During his minority it was jointly held by Thomas Fiennes and Thomas Oxenbridge. When Thomas did succeed, as Thomas Lord Dacre, he spent a lifetime in loyal service to the crown. In turn he was succeeded in 1533 by his grandson, another Thomas, who suffered an inglorious death by execution in 1541 for murder, at the age of twenty-four.

This Thomas Dacre was something of a high-spirited individual and one night decided to play a prank on his neighbour, Sir Nicholas Pelham, with whom he had recently fallen out. Dacre, along with his friends George Roydon, John Frowdys and John Mantell, rode off to the Pelham estate to hunt Sir Nicholas's deer. It was apparently a bright, moonlit night, and they were spotted in their exploit by Pelham's gamekeeper, who was patrolling the park with two companions.

The gamekeeper ordered Dacre and his friends to leave the property, but instead they drew their swords and gave chase to him. The high jinks got out of hand, tempers became frayed, and a fight broke out between them. The gamekeeper fell to the ground from a sword wound, believed to have been delivered by Dacre himself, and suddenly the fun was over. Dacre and his men made a hurried retreat and the two companions carried the wounded man back to Sir Nicholas Pelham's house.

45. Aerial view of Herstmonceux taken during the last war (note the camouflaged huts). The grounds have been considerably beautified with extensive plantings since then.

The gamekeeper died as a result of his wound, but not before telling his master who his murderers were. Pelham, an extremely powerful man of his day, had Lord Dacre and his three associates arrested for murder. They were all duly found guilty and later executed.

On Thomas Dacre's execution, Herstmonceux castle and its lands were forfeited to the crown, along with the title, but both were restored to Gregory Dacre in 1558 by Elizabeth I. Gregory was Thomas Dacre's second eldest son, who succeeded when Thomas, the eldest son, died while the estate was still in forfeiture. In 1604 his sister Margaret succeeded to the estate, claiming to be the rightful heir. She was allowed to remain at Herstmonceux, but only by grant from the king. The castle thus remained in Dacre hands for a further four generations.

The last Lord Dacre, another Thomas, was allowed to succeed to the estate providing he paid a dowry of £20,000 and married Lady Anne Fitzroy, daughter of the Duchess of Cleveland. Dacre, created Earl of Sussex by Charles II, had still not paid the dowry by 1692 so an order was issued by the king allowing him to sell off part of his estates. Dacre was a compulsive gambler and indulged himself in frivolous behaviour at Court. He fell heavily into debt and when, shortly before his death, he sold Herstmonceux castle to repay some of this money, it was then suffering badly from neglect. The purchaser was a Mr. George Naylor, who bought it in 1708 for £38,215.

Next it passed to Dr. Francis Hare, Bishop of Chichester, who claimed he could not afford the upkeep of the place. On his death in 1775 Herstmonceux passed to his son, the Rev. Robert Hare, who likewise found the cost of its upkeep too high. His wife, Henrietta, persuaded him to dismantle the interior and use the materials to construct additional rooms in a new, more fashionable house they were building elsewhere in the park. So it was that, in 1777, the interior of the castle was gutted for the sake of its materials. The exterior was left virtually intact, providing a romantic feature for the park. An Elizabethan survey revealed that the moat had to be drained—for health reasons—but that the castle itself was in excellent condition. By the time of its demolition, however, the condition of the interior buildings at least had deteriorated dramatically, and most of the timber was much decayed.

In 1807 the castle was sold for £60,000 to Thomas Read Kemp, M.P. for Lewes and owner of Lewes castle, but it remained largely a ruin until Colonel Claude Lowther purchased it in 1911. He consolidated the structure and carried out some basic restoration. When he died in 1929 it was bought by Reginald Lawrence Lawson, who in turn sold it to Sir Paul Latham in 1932. A year later, Sir Paul, with his

46. A rare photograph (dated 1891) taken from the south-east, showing Herstmonceux prior to restoration.

architect, Walter Godfrey, embarked on a massive restoration and rebuilding programme. The results of their efforts are to be seen today in the present castle.

The exterior was not altered during the restoration, save for necessary repairs, and the remaining original features from the interior were incorporated into the new buildings of the courtyard. The restoration was indeed exemplary, for it is now almost impossible to detect the 20th-century work from that of the 15th century. The only substantial deviation from the previous internal arrangement was the decision to build the new apartments around one central courtyard. The castle is now the curious victim of modern bureaucracy. The interior, which is classified as being of modern construction, is wholly the responsibility of the Royal Greenwich Observatory, its present owners, but the exterior is listed as an ancient monument by the Department of the Environment and responsibility for its upkeep rests solely with them.

The Royal Observatory was founded at Greenwich in 1675 by Charles II and is the oldest scientific institution in Britain. However, as London grew the skies above the observatory became polluted, making observation extremely difficult. In 1939 it was decided to move the observatory to a country location, and Herstmonceux, in Sussex, was the site eventually chosen. In 1948 the Royal Observatory moved in, setting up their telescopes and other equipment in purpose-built buildings in the grounds and taking over the castle itself as their administrative and residential centre. Unfortunately, the castle interior

is not open to view, except for two rooms housing an exhibition relating the history of both the observatory and the castle.

The grounds are open to the public and they are exquisitely beautiful, famed for the large variety of wildlife there. The original walled Elizabethan gardens were restored by Sir Paul Latham and extended by him to include a lavender garden and a rhododendron dell. Much of what the visitor sees today, however, is the result of plantings since the Royal Observatory moved in. They maintain the grounds and surrounding parkland partly for aesthetic reasons and partly to assist in their observations. The planting of many hundreds of acres with trees and shrubs helps to reduce air turbulence around the telescopes—the most important of which is the famous Isaac Newton telescope. The principle telescopes are soon to be moved to the more favourable conditions of the Canary Islands, but the observatory will continue to use the Herstmonceux site.

Visitors are well catered for and the grounds form an idyllic picnic spot. From every vantage point, the eye is continually drawn to the obvious centre-piece—the magnificent castle. The moat, which only half encircles the castle, is lake-like in expanse and reflects in its quiet waters the utter perfection of Sir Roger Fiennes's battlemented home. In the grounds is an avenue of Spanish chestnuts. When one of these was felled in 1979 through disease it was found to be 229 years old. A slice of the trunk has been polished and forms a unique display of various events in the castle's history marked against the appropriate annual rings of the tree.

Akin to Bodiam for the romance of its setting, Herstmonceux nonetheless plays host to an astonishing number of spectres. These include a 9ft. tall drummer who accompanied Sir Roger on the field at Agincourt. His, and the drumming of another ghost, that of one of the Lord Dacres, still haunt the castle. Ironically, Dacre imitated the soldier's drumming to frighten off would-be admirers of his young wife and now he, too, haunts the castle. Lady Grace Naylor haunts a part of the castle known as the 'Ladies' Bower', where she was starved to death to prevent her from inheriting Herstmonceux. Finally, Thomas Dacre and his three associates, who murdered the unfortunate gamekeeper, are reputed to haunt the castle grounds at midnight on the anniversary of their deed; a grim reminder that all is not necessarily what it seems.

47.   Knepp Old Castle: the ruins look, from a distance, to be of a circular tower, but are in fact the remains of a single wall of a rectangular keep.

Knepp

(Cnap. Cnappe. Kneppe. Knob, or knoll of land.)

The sombre remains of Knepp (old) castle, standing alongside the Worthing–Horsham road, cannot fail to catch one's eye. Yet, just as the modern-day traveller motors past in a few seconds, so, too, does its story flash upon the page of the history of Sussex for a few brief moments and then is gone. The ruins today consist of but one fragment of wall, part of the keep, standing about 30ft. high on a large, shallow mound, similar in shape to a giant-size upturned saucer.

What we know of its history is closely linked to Bramber castle; so, too, was its fate. It seems to have been of some importance as a secondary residence of the de Braose family of Bramber, who built it. When lands in this part of Sussex were divided after the Conquest, a grant from the king to William de Braose refers to a 'manor and park of Cnap', its more familiar spelling in old documents.

While no masonry from the curtain wall and other defences survives, it can be reasonably inferred from a study of the earthworks that the castle was circular in form, enclosing about two acres and covering the entire crest of the surviving mound. Aerial photographs seem to confirm this and suggest that the castle consisted of this one, circular bailey, for no evidence of further earthworks has so far been discovered. Separate branches of the river Adur pass by on either side of the mound and it is reasonable to assume that they once fed a wet moat surrounding the castle.

The mound itself may be of prehistoric origin and a Saxon fortress may have preceded the castle, but neither of these points has yet been proven. It can be presumed, however, that William de Braose, first Norman lord of Bramber, erected Knepp castle at the same time as he built his principal residence at Bramber itself, in the early or mid-12th century. Whether or not Knepp castle simply constituted an occasional hunting-seat of the de Braoses is not certain. While the castle was large enough to be considered a true castle in its own right and not merely a solitary tower, as was Verdley castle, Knepp remained attached to the Rape and Honour of Bramber, passing down the same line of descent. The de Braoses seem to have been in frequent residence at Knepp, for many letters were written from there.

Knepp castle passed out of their hands, along with Bramber and all their other estates, during the reign of King John. In 1208 John, fearing William de Braose was plotting with the other barons against him, sent a letter to Matilda, his wife, requesting that she entrust the custody of her children to the king. John's reason for such a strange request was no doubt to ensure de Braose's loyalty, for he would hardly rebel against him with his children held as hostages. Matilda sent an indignant reply to John, refusing to comply with his wishes and soon after fled to Ireland with her children. Two years passed and John eventually learned of their whereabouts. They were betrayed and brought back to England, where they were imprisoned in Windsor castle and later starved to death. William de Braose, who had not accompanied his family to Ireland, died a few years later in France where he had presumably gone to enlist the help of the French barons.

48. Knepp Old Castle: close-up view of the keep showing some early herringbone work.

John immediately seized the opportunity to take possession of all of de Braoses lands and estates, among them the castle of Knepp, which he gave to his son, the Duke of Cornwall. He stayed at the castle on at least four occasions, in April 1206, May 1209, in 1211, and in January 1215. Queen Isabella was at Knepp for 11 days over Christmas in 1214-15. John issued a number of letters and documents whilst at the castle, including one dated 1211 in which he confirmed the grants of benefactors to Bayham abbey.

Knepp castle became something of a favourite for King John, who used it more as a hunting seat than a castle. To this end he stored a huge quantity of supplies within its walls and continually kept the surrounding park stocked with game. He issued an order in 1214 that the castle was to be fortified for fear its contents (mainly hunting equipment, which he considered to be of paramount importance) should fall into the hands of the insurgent barons. By now the political climate in England had turned completely against John. In this year the Pope sanctioned Prince Louis of France to seize the English throne, a move welcomed by many English barons. Less than two years later John, fearing the worst and feeling his reign as king was irretrievably lost, wrote the following letter to the Sheriff of Sussex, a certain Roland Bloett, whom he had installed at Knepp castle:

> The King to Roland Bloett greeting—
>
> Know ye that the Citizens of London gave up their City to our enimis, quickly and of their own free will, on the Sunday after the feast of St. Dunstan. Therefore we command you to carry away from Cnap, and elsewhere all that can be removed, and to take it without delay to Bramber, and secure it in the House there, unless you can better bestow it in the castle; but the House at Cnap you shall totally destroy.
>
> Signed by me at Fremantle, May 18th. [1216].

One cannot but feel sorry for John when reading this letter, despite his tyrannical rule, for between the lines one senses the sheer desperation to which he had been driven. But he died before the crown could be wrested from him and so was spared the final indignity of being deposed by force. There are, however, suspicious circumstances surrounding his death. Louis was packed off to France by the barons and the infant Prince Henry placed on the throne. Knepp castle apparently was not destroyed, as John had instructed, for Henry III later carried out repairs to it and used it as an occasional residence.

Henry III also reinstated Reginald de Braose in 1218 to the Bramber estates which included Knepp castle, not as any kind of recompense for the way his father had treated the de Braose family, but rather to ensure his allegiance in the barons' wars of his day. Knepp continued

49. An 18th-century print of the ruins of Knepp Old Castle by S. Hooper (dated 1776).

in occasional use by the de Braoses, but by 1282 it was in the
possession of a family who took their name from the estate, the
de la Cnaps, who may have been distantly related to the de Braoses.
There the recorded history of Knepp castle ends. It is likely that it
fell from use both as a castle and a residence at the beginning of the
14th century. It afterwards suffered the ignoble fate of being dismantled during the 18th and later centuries for its materials to be
used to build roads. The estates later passed to the Mowbray, Seymour,
Nye and Caryll families, the last of whom sold them in 1752 to
William Belcher. He in turn sold them to the Burrells who were
responsible for building the 'new' castle at Knepp.

50. The splendid barbican and outer gatehouse, Lewes Castle, viewed from the top of the mound.

Lewes

(Laewe. Laewas. Lewis. From hlaew, a prominent or grave hill.)

Little is known of the early history of Lewes before the Norman Conquest, but afterwards it became the administrative centre of one of the six Rapes of Sussex. It was granted to William de Warenne, who married Gundrada, long thought to be one of the Conqueror's daughters, but doubt on her parentage has recently been cast. De Warenne was nonetheless a man of some importance and in addition he was granted large parcels of land in Surrey and Norfolk. He was appointed Chief Justiciar and played a leading role in putting down the rebellion of Roger, Earl of Hereford, during one of the Conqueror's frequent absences. He also founded a Cluniac priory in Lewes following a visit with his wife to the Abbey of Cluny in Burgundy.

The castle he built at Lewes is remarkable for two reasons: it possesses two mounds instead of the usual one and displays herringbone masonry datable to the last years of the 11th century. A possible reason for the presence of two mounds may lie in the natural features of the land itself. Although both are artificially constructed of chalk blocks, at their cores are small natural hillocks providing a convenient nucleus for the mounds to be built. The smaller of the two, the Brack Mount, is traditionally believed to contain a burial, though none has been found, and both may date from prehistoric times, to be adapted later by the Normans for defensive purposes. When he arrived at Lewes, de Warenne strengthened the mounds and pared away the ground at their bases and on the level land between them to form a sharp escarpment. The mound nearest the town was provided with a shell keep, while the Brack Mount appears simply to have been protected by a curtain wall running up two of its sides to the summit. A fragment of flint walling can still be seen near the top.

Gundrada died in 1085 at Castle Acre, one of the de Warenne's Norfolk strongholds, but her body was brought back to Sussex and buried at Lewes priory. De Warenne supported Rufus when the Conqueror died in 1087, and was consequently created Earl of Surrey, but at the siege of Pevensey castle the following year he was mortally

51. Aerial view showing the mound, Lewes Castle, with its attendant shell keep, and barbican. The levelled space was once the castle courtyard and the Brack Mount lies just beyond the clump of trees at the top of the photograph.

wounded. He died on 24 June 1088 leaving two sons and three daughters. His body was buried at the priory alongside Gundrada's, but in the 12th century the monks re-interred them both at St John's church, Southover, where they remain.

William's eldest son, also William, still a minor when he succeeded as the 2nd Earl, remained loyal to Rufus. When the king died in 1100 William de Warenne supported Robert, the Conqueror's eldest son, but the younger son, Henry, eventually won his claim, taking the English throne by force. Henry I dispossessed de Warenne of his Surrey estates for supporting Robert, but allowed him to keep his Sussex properties. It is some indication of the rapidly changing loyalties of the Middle Ages that we next hear of de Warenne being reinstated to his lost estates and in 1106 fighting alongside King Henry when Robert was finally defeated at the siege of Tenchebrai. In addition, de Warenne became an ardent supporter of the king in protecting his

Norman dominions and remained a close confidant until Henry's death in 1135. Before he himself died in 1138, de Warenne completed the building of Lewes and Castle Acre priories and further extended Lewes castle.

His son, yet another William, succeeded as 3rd Earl and seems to have followed his father in changing his loyalties according to the prevailing wind in the power struggles for the English throne. He started in support of Stephen's claim to the crown, changed sides when Stephen's fortunes changed, but joined him again in 1141 at the Battle of Lincoln. Stephen was defeated and taken prisoner at the battle so de Warenne switched his allegiance yet again to Matilda. In a subsequent battle, however, he himself was taken prisoner by Stephen and later died on crusade in 1147. Rainwald de Warenne, William's brother, held Lewes in his absence, and on his death ended the line of direct male heirs to the earldom.

It was common in medieval times, when the last direct male heir to an estate died and the property passed to a female heir, for her husband to assume her family name if it carried more importance. This accounts for the apparent continuity of many prominent families and estates, which in reality passed through several different male lines. This happened at Lewes, for when Rainwald died he left his estates to his daughter Isabel. She married the youngest son of King Stephen, William de Blois, who thus became heir to the titles Earl of Surrey and Warenne, though he was still only 12 years old.

De Blois was a close friend of Matilda's son, later to become Henry II, and when both his father and elder brother died he made no attempt to contest Henry's claim to the English throne. He remained a close friend of the king and was knighted by him in 1158. When he died the following year at the age of only 25 he had amassed incredible power, including the Honour of Pevensey and the titles of Count of Boulogne and of Mortain, in addition to his inherited properties at Lewes and Norwich. In 1162 de Blois's widow married the illegitimate son of Geoffrey of Anjou, Hameline Plantagenet, half-brother of King Henry II. Once again the estates and earldom passed, by marriage, to the husband of the female heir, Isabel. She died in 1199, followed three years later by Hameline, leaving a son, William, to succeed as 6th Earl.

When King John lost his French possessions, his barons, who held the land from the king in the usual way, likewise lost their estates. By way of compensation John was forced to give the more important barons additional lands and titles in England. William, 6th Earl Warenne, was granted Grantham and Stamford, and was said to have introduced bear-baiting to the latter.

De Warenne supported John in the barons' wars, though more to suit his own ends than from any sense of duty or loyalty. He was instrumental in drafting the king's acceptance of Magna Carta and amply secured his own position in the process. In 1216 he was created Warden of the Cinque Ports, and was Sheriff of Surrey between 1217 and 1226. He played a prominent role in politics for the rest of his life, taking part in both the Welsh and French wars. When John died, leaving his son Henry as heir to the throne (though still a boy), de Warenne gave his allegiance to the king. He greatly added to his estates by marrying first, Maud, daughter of William, Earl of Arundel, and then the daughter of William Marshall, Earl of Pembroke, another Maud. She was also the widow of the Earl of Norfolk, Hugh le Bigod. When he died in 1240 his son, John, was just four years old.

Peter of Savoy, Queen Eleanor's uncle, held Lewes during John's minority. Later, in the barons' wars of Henry III's reign, he fervently fought at first on the king's side, only to switch his support to the barons. In keeping with family tradition, however, he returned to the king's side and helped in the defence of Rochester castle against Simon de Montfort. In May 1264 the decisive Battle of Lewes was fought at a site just outside the town. The royal troops were defeated, de Warenne fled from the battle and escaped to France. The victorious de Montfort banished him, and gave his estates, except the castles of Reigate and Lewes, to Gilbert, Earl of Gloucester. In 1265 de Warenne returned to England and fought alongside the king at the Battle of Evesham, where Simon de Montfort was defeated and killed. De Montfort's cause had not been in vain, however, for he laid the foundations on which our present democratic parliament is built. John de Warenne's estates were restored to him by Henry III, with the additional title of Earl of Sussex.

He took part in Edward I's Scottish wars, becoming Commander-in-Chief at Trent, Constable of Bamburgh castle, Guardian and Lieutenant of Scotland, and fought with the king at the siege of Caerlaverock castle in 1300. He died in 1305 at the age of 70, after a full and active political life. His only son, William, had died in a tournament some years before in 1285 leaving two daughters. This time, however, the earldom did not pass by marriage to another male line, but went instead to his grandson John, even though he, too, was still a minor. He married Joan de Bar, one of Edward I's granddaughters. He was a soldier of distinction in the Scottish wars of Edward III and was created Earl of Strathearne. He was once excommunicated by the Church because of his infidelities, but when he died in 1347 the decision must have been reversed, for he was buried in Lewes priory.

He left no legitimate heirs, so on his death all his possessions passed to Richard Fitzalan, 13th Earl of Arundel and de Warenne's nephew.

52. Lewes Castle: the mound and shell keep, erected in the late 11th and early 12th century.

Once again the direct line of ownership of Lewes castle ended leaving it without a resident lord. Fitzalan spent most of his time at Arundel castle, but he stayed at Lewes from time to time, as extant letters written from there by him demonstrate. Lewes castle remained in this situation until 1382, when the townspeople broke in, causing substantial damage to the fabric. Afterwards the Earls of Arundel ceased to use Lewes as a residence; instead it became a storehouse for wool. By the beginning of the 15th century Lewes castle, which had never been successfully attacked, was left to moulder in ruins. For a castle that grew from such beginnings to one of the foremost seats in the land, such an end is indeed ignominious.

In 1620 much of the castle was pulled down and its stone sold for building materials. The castle bailey, or green, was used later for public meetings. Daniel Defoe, writing in 1725, remarked that some of the apartments were repaired and made habitable, and later part of the keep was converted into a summer house. In 1733 the barbican (and in 1750 the keep) was granted to Thomas Friend, a wool merchant who lived in nearby Barbican House. They then passed to Thomas Read Kemp, whose grandfather had carried out the alterations to the keep.

In 1850 the Sussex Archaeological Society moved in, first as tenants and, after 1922, as owners. The Society still owns the castle keep, gatehouse and Barbican House, which are held in trust, and uses the latter as a museum to exhibit finds made during their excavations. The other portions of the castle were divided and sold off separately. A road now passes through the middle of the castle, a number of houses stand on the sites of the various outbuildings, a bowling green occupies the former bailey area, and the Brack Mount is now completely detached from the rest. Fragments of the other castle buildings survive, but the principle remains are those of the keep, gatehouse and barbican, the parts administered by the Sussex Archaeological Society.

The castle stands on raised ground just north of the High Street and commands the valley of the river Ouse. The area enclosed between its two mounds is approximately 450ft. by 380ft. The larger, south-west mound, stands about 65ft. high above the level of the High Street and about 130ft. above the level of the plain upon which the town stands. The Brack Mount is about 20ft. lower. The earthworks which once connected the two mounds are now mostly obliterated by the buildings of the modern town.

In the late 11th, or early 12th, century an elliptical shell keep was erected on top of the south-western mound and was further protected in the 13th century by the addition of two semi-octagonal towers. These towers, which present five sides to the field and one wide flat side to the interior, and the southern half of the keep survive in good condition. A latrine shaft, a large fireplace and a curious shaft passing through the wall are to be seen within the keep, and on display are a set of stocks and an ancient British canoe.

53. Internal view of the shell keep, Lewes Castle, showing one of the 13th-century towers.

A substantial part of the Norman gatehouse also survives behind the barbican, which was erected in front of it by John, 7th Earl Warenne, in about 1330. The barbican is undoubtedly the most impressive part of the castle, and its gateway still straddles the road in near perfect condition. The lower levels are roughly rectangular, but the two projecting towers are circular, rising from the angles in the manner of bartizans. The flint work is of exceptional quality. The parapet projects outwards on a row of machicolations and was restored, with the west tower, in 1895.

The keep is of exceptional interest and well worth the long climb up the mound. The impressive doorways into the towers are of fairly recent construction, but everything else is original. An excellent display is housed in the two upper floors of the south tower, consisting of four illuminated panels outlining in graphic detail the history of both the castle and town. From the battlements of this tower there is a magnificent view of the town and surrounding countryside. A unique feature here, between the merlons of the battlements, is seven 'view-finder' panels—metal plaques with descriptive sketches etched on them, pointing out various buildings of interest to be seen from each position. This is an admirable indication of the farsightedness and interest with which the Sussex Archaeological Society cares for this impressive castle and caters for its many visitors.

54.   Standing on the site of a great medieval ca
Petworth House is best seen from across the wie
expanse of the lake in the surrounding park.

Petworth House

(Peteorde. Peteswurda. Putteworth. Peota's worth, or enclosure.)

Petworth House today gives no outward indication of its origins as a medieval castle, yet the observant visitor wandering among its rooms will detect clues which reveal its antiquity. The chapel is the oldest part of the existing house and dates from the 13th century.

The first settlement at Petworth, however, is believed to date from the late 5th or early 6th century, when a Saxon settler (Peota) established a farmstead there on a hill in the vast forest that covered most of Sussex. Immediately before the Conquest it was held by King Harold's sister, Edith, Edward the Confessor's queen. After the Conquest the manor of Petworth was given to Roger de Montgomery, who elected Robert Fitzbald to hold it for him. Later Henry I conferred it on his second wife, Adeliza, who in turn gave it to her brother, Joscelyn de Louvain. When he married Lady Agnes de Percy in 1150 Petworth thus passed into the possession of the wealthy and influential Percy family, Earls of Northumberland. Lady Agnes was the great-grand-daughter of William de Percy, a favourite of the Conqueror, who had come over with him in 1066. De Percy was richly rewarded for his services and was given huge parcels of land throughout the kingdom, making him one of the most powerful nobles in England after the king.

It is not known whether the first Percy household at Petworth was ever fortified, but it was certainly a very substantial structure. In 1309 Henry Lord Percy received a licence to crenellate this house, which then became one of the most important Percy strongholds in the south. Unfortunately, nothing is known of the original layout of this castle, for the site has been completely rebuilt, but one imagines it to have been comparable with their other castles in the north, such as Alnwick and Warkworth. The Percys were for many years at the heart of political intrigue in this country, and no less than seven Earls of Northumberland died violent deaths through battle or murder, execution, or imprisonment. The 6th Earl was perhaps even more unfortunate, for he died of a broken heart having had the misfortune to fall in love with Anne Boleyn when Henry VIII was seeking her favours.

55. A 19th-century engraving of Petworth House viewed from across the park. The spire is not part of the house, but belongs to the parish church, immediately adjacent to the park wall.

Henry, 9th Earl, also fell upon hard times. A learned and well-read man, he was also a patron of the arts and spent a lifetime collecting books and various artefacts. He was implicated, with other members of his family, in the Gunpowder Plot, and was imprisoned in the Tower of London for 16 years. Eventually he was released in 1621 on payment of a colossal £11,000 fine. He acquired the nickname 'The Wizard Earl' because he spent the last years of his life in the cellars of the new wing he built at Petworth for experiments in science and alchemy.

His son Algernon, 10th Earl, also resided for many years at Petworth, extending both the castle and his father's art collection. In the Civil War he gained the respect of both parliamentarians and royalists, and at one stage even looked after the younger children of Charles I on parliament's behalf. Algernon died in 1668. Two years later the untimely death of his son Joscelyn, aged only 26, meant that the entire Percy estates passed to an only daughter, Elizabeth, then still a child.

The hapless Elizabeth led a miserable life, married off by her scheming grandmother no less than three times before her 16th birthday. Her three husbands were first, the Duke of Newcastle, who died in 1680 without issue; second, Thomas Thynne of Longleat, mysteriously murdered in London in 1681; and third, Charles Seymour, 6th Duke of Somerset, whom she married in 1682 and to whose family Petworth then passed. Seymour was a proud, conceited and arrogant man, obsessed with his lineage and with his own rank in society. The combination of his own estates with the Percys' served only to fuel his conceit, earning him the title of the 'Proud Duke'. He is reputed to have sent servants ahead of his coach when travelling to clear 'common folk' off the road.

The 'old fashioned' Percy house at Petworth, by then a mixture of Jacobean mansion and medieval castle, proved too humble a residence for Seymour so he decided to demolish it. He erected in its place a new and more gracious house between 1688–96. As a result practically all trace of the castle has disappeared. Apart from the chapel, already mentioned, the only surviving relics are some of the cellars and the undercroft of the medieval great hall. Petworth House, the 'gracious' mansion erected on its site and described in the official guide as a 'late 17th-century Baroque Palace', is a large but otherwise plain house built in the French manner.

Externally it is undistinguished but, viewed from across the lake in the surrounding parkland, the west front is very impressive and carries with it a certain elegance. The park, landscaped by Capability Brown, and gardens are magnificent, however, forming an idyllic and picturesque surround. A mound situated between the house and lake may once have formed part of the original castle defences, or it may be part of Brown's landscaping.

The real beauty of Petworth House lies not in its architecture, but in the excellence of its interior. The stately rooms are sumptuously decorated and contain a wealth of fine furnishings and artefacts. The grand staircase is undoubtedly the showpiece. It consists almost entirely of plain walls and ceiling, but so expertly have they been painted by Laguerre in vivid three-dimensional effect that the results are quite overwhelming. Petworth is famed today of course for possessing one of the finest private collections of paintings in England, including many of Turner's works. Turner stayed at Petworth on occasion and painted a number of his landscapes whilst there, including some of the park.

From the Seymour–Percy family line Petworth then passed to the Wyndhams, Earls of Egremont, who delighted in entertaining royalty. In one year alone, 1814, Petworth was visited by the Tsar of Russia, the King of Prussia, and the Prince Regent, among other royal personages. The earldom became extinct, however, when in 1837 the 3rd Earl, Lord Egremont, for some curious reason omitted to marry his wife until after the births of his six children. The earldom passed to his nephew and soon after died out.

Petworth is now the property of the National Trust, given to them by the 3rd Lord Leconfield in 1947. The present Lord Egremont (a Wyndham) still resides in part of the house, however, thus continuing the long Percy–Seymour–Wyndham sequence that began when Petworth was a true castle.

56. Looking through one of the immensely long arrow-loops
(eight feet) in one of the 13th-century drum towers, Pevensey.

Pevensey

(Roman, Anderida, Pefenesea. Pevensye. Pefen's marshland.)

The south-east coast of England has long been termed the 'Invasion Coast'. This tiny corner stretching from Pevensey in Sussex to Deal in Kent has borne the brunt of most foreign invasions of this land, as recently as the proposed German landing in the Second World War. Pevensey itself has witnessed the arrival of Roman, Saxon, Danish and Norman invaders. It was here that on 28 September 1066 Duke William landed with his army from Normandy to lay claim to the throne of England. Two weeks later the decisive Battle of Hastings was fought and lost by the English at Senlac Hill, a mere 10 miles distant. The Bayeux Tapestry records the event for us thus: 'Here Duke William in a great ship crossed the sea and came to Pevensey'.

When the Normans arrived at Pevensey they found the mouldering and deserted ruins of a Roman fort which they made use of as a base from which to launch their attack. They hurriedly carried out some basic repairs to it, in timber, to make the place defensible. In the course of the next few days its harbour, which was still in use, was used to land all the necessary troops and supplies for the invasion, including prefabricated wooden panels for temporary 'castles' acting as military rallying points. Later the timber defences inside Pevensey fort were replaced in stone, forming the substantial castle we see today, and the Roman walls were repaired. Despite a long history of neglect, this fortress was again called into action to defend the 'Invasion Coast' when gun emplacements were positioned within the ancient walls to repel Hitler's intended invasion.

The Roman fort at Pevensey was built around A.D. 340 and was one of the chain of forts along the south and east coasts to repel raids by Saxon pirates. There were at least nine, possibly eleven forts in this chain, which came to be known collectively as 'The Roman forts of the Saxon shore'. Four of the forts were in neighbouring Kent at Dover, Lympne, Richborough and Reculver. The commander in charge of the forts was known as the 'Count of the Saxon shore'.

In recent years, however, a new school of thought has emerged to question the reasons behind the construction of the forts. Most of the

57. View of the Roman fort at Pevensey, from an old engraving, showing one of the original entrance gates.

chain was already completed by about 280, long before Saxon raids were considered a threat to Roman rule in Britain. Pevensey is the only one that can be said with certainty to have been erected to repel the Saxons. In about 286 Carausius set himself up as Emperor of Britain in defiance of Rome, and it is possible that he built the forts to repel an attack from Rome itself, in an attempt to re-conquer Britain. The re-invasion, if it can be so called, did take place under Maximian, and in later years the forts were probably used to protect the coast against the Saxons, whose raids had increased in both frequency and ferocity.

The shape of the fort at Pevensey is most uncharacteristic of Roman forts, which usually comprised a rigidly symmetrical square or rectangular enclosure with bastions placed at regular intervals along the walls. Pevensey, however, is oval and the towers are irregularly spaced. The reason for this deviation from the Roman norm lies in the nature of the land on which the fort is built. In Roman times it formed a narrow, oval-shaped peninsula which jutted out into the sea, and so provided a safe shelter for ships. The walls of the fort followed the outline of the peninsula, which was also marshland and prevented the Romans from imposing their usual symmetrical shape upon it. The sea has long since receded and the marshland reclaimed, silting up the accompanying harbour and leaving the fort high and dry in the midst of lush farmland. Three important Roman roads led from the fort to Dover, Portsmouth and London, the routes of which are still in use today.

The *Anglo-Saxon Chronicle* tells us that in the year 491 a large number of Britons, who were sheltering within the Roman walls of Pevensey, were massacred by the Saxons under Ella. We are told that

58. Aerial view showing the unusual oval shape of the Roman fort, with the medieval castle of Pevensey in its south-eastern corner. The stretch of wall beneath the line of trees, to the right of the picture, has largely collapsed.

not a single Briton was left alive. Soon after the fort was deserted, and not permanently inhabited again until Duke William's arrival in 1066. The Normans met no opposition at Pevensey and soon secured the fort. After the Conquest, William divided Sussex into six strips, or rapes, one of which was centred around Pevensey. He gave Pevensey to his half-brother, Robert, Count of Mortain, who founded a small township outside the fort. He established a castle within the fort by sectioning off the south-east corner by means of a ditch and rampart. A timber palisade was erected on top of this rampart. The Roman walls of the fort, which thus formed a large outer bailey some 10 acres in extent, were repaired in stone.

During the turbulent years of William II's (Rufus) reign, an attempt was made by Robert of Mortain and his brother, Odo, Bishop of Bayeux, to place Robert, Duke of Normandy on the English throne. Robert was, of course, the Conqueror's eldest son and considered he had a stronger claim to the English throne than his brother, Rufus. In 1088 Robert of Mortain and Odo held Pevensey against William Rufus, who succeeded in taking the castle, not by force but by starving the garrison into submission.

Pevensey next passed to William, Count of Mortain who, in 1101, rebelled against Henry I in the power struggle between the Dukes of Normandy and the Kings of England. He was unsuccessful and was made to hand over Pevensey castle to the crown. Henry I granted it to Richer de Aquila and in Stephen's reign it was held by Gilbert de Aquila, Earl of Pembroke. He, too, rebelled against the king, in 1147. The walls of Pevensey again proved too strong to submit to direct assault, but Stephen eventually starved the garrison to defeat. He gave the castle and Rape to his eldest son, Eustace, and when he died prematurely, to his younger son, William, Earl of Warenne.

When Henry II succeeded to the throne in 1154 Pevensey was surrendered to him and he returned it to Gilbert de Aquila, whom he considered to be its rightful owner. Another Gilbert rebelled against King John and supported Prince Louis of France. Once again the castle was forfeited to the crown, but on reaffirming his allegiance to Henry III, it was restored to him. By this time the castle had been re-fortified in stone throughout and acquired a massive keep, making it a fortress of quite considerable power. It passed back to the crown once more and was subsequently granted to Peter de Rivallis, Earl of Hereford.

In 1240 it was surrendered by Gilbert Marshall, Earl of Pembroke, to the crown yet again, and six years later it was granted to Peter of Savoy, Earl of Richmond. He was responsible for carrying out a massive rebuilding programme, reducing the extent of the inner bailey to its present size and erecting the three drum towers. He did not stay long at Pevensey, however, and returned to his native Savoy.

The castle withstood a third siege in 1264–65 following the defeat of Henry III's supporters by the barons at Lewes. The fleeing royalists took refuge in Pevensey where they were immediately pursued by the barons under Simon de Montfort the younger. A ferocious siege took place, but the castle held firm and the barons had to withdraw their forces. A large number of stone ammunition balls, used in medieval siege engines, has been discovered at Pevensey during restoration. The royal accounts show that Pevensey was in possession of at least one large stone-throwing engine and many of the balls are

probably part of the castle's ammunition store, but some may well
have been fired by the barons during the siege of 1265.

As with Leeds castle, in Kent, it became a tradition in the Middle
Ages to grant Pevensey to the queens of England, who became
personally responsible for the appointment of constables. This custom
continued until 1372 when the castle was given to John of Gaunt.
His son, Henry, Duke of Lancaster, is noted in history for laying claim
to the throne of England in 1399. The result of this confrontation was
that Pevensey had to withstand yet another siege, this time conducted
by Richard II. Sir John Pelham, the Constable, had left to fight with
the Duke of Lancaster's army, leaving his wife, Lady Joan, to defend
the castle in his absence. By this time Pevensey's defences were very
much in need of repair, but Lady Joan managed to hold out until
relieved by the duke's troops. After Henry had placed himself on the
throne as Henry IV, Sir John Pelham continued as Constable, and
many very important prisoners were entrusted to his care, including
James I of Scotland.

Pevensey castle declined greatly in importance as the sea receded,
a process accelerated by land reclamation in the area. Gradually the
harbour silted up and the marshes became lush meadowland. This
sounded the death knell for Pevensey castle long before the advent
of cannons, so that what was once one of the main centres of population in medieval Sussex rapidly declined to form the pleasant village
we see now.

59. The Roman West gate, Pevensey Castle. Although similar in appearance to
medieval towers, Roman towers were usually built solid to wall-walk level.

Because Pevensey was a royal castle for most of its active life it was totally reliant on the crown for revenue to effect repairs to its fabric. Consequently, a brief study of the Exchequer accounts shows how often Pevensey was sorely in need of repair. An indication of its decline in importance can be found as early as 1250 when licence was sought to remove the church from within the castle and rebuild it in the outer enclosure of the fort for the use of the townspeople. The implication was that the ancient Roman walls were no longer maintained as part of the castle, but were regarded as a town wall.

Throughout their history the Roman walls required constant attention, and large sections frequently collapsed from landslips in the marshy ground. During the siege of 1264-65 Simon de Montfort destroyed a long length of the walls which seems never to have been repaired. In 1302 and 1318 two more sections fell down near the castle, later to be repaired, but further falls to the north rendered the keep in a ruinous state as early as the opening years of the 15th century.

That the castle had soon fallen into a state of disrepair is supported by another entry in the Exchequer accounts shortly after 1306, stating that the steps and bridge to the keep had collapsed. Shortly after that the timber floors and roofs of the keep and north tower had also fallen. Immediate repairs were carried out to retain the castle in some kind of defensive state, but its history is one of continued negligence brought about by its declining strategic importance.

Despite this negligence and deliberate destruction in later years for building materials, the castle and fort today are in splendid condition. About three-quarters of the Roman fort still stands to a considerable height. It is built of stone and flint with brick lacing courses of very high quality. The walls revet a raised platform giving a higher ground level inside the fort than outside, and consequently appear higher and more impressive from the outside. A public footpath passes through the fort from east to west and is freely accessible.

The medieval castle in the south-east corner of the fort (for which an admission charge is made) is similarly impressive and of a high standard of construction. Parts of Robert of Mortain's castle survive in the gatehouse, but most of the present remains (the three D-shaped towers and connecting curtain wall) date from the mid–13th century. The three drum towers contain immensely long arrow loops about eight feet in length. The keep has been reduced to its lower levels only and presents a most confusing conglomeration of stonework. Originally it consisted of a standard rectangular Norman keep measuring

30. Internal view of the gatehouse, Pevensey Castle, from across the courtyard. The cannon is an Elizabethan demi-culverin.

55ft. by 30ft. internally. The apsidal projections are believed to have been added in the 13th century for additional strength or to mount siege engines, such as trebuchets.

In the vaulted basements of the two towers of the gatehouse are two very curious apartments. That in the south tower is reached by a spiral staircase in the thickness of the wall, that in the north is accessible only by a trap door in the roof of its vault—at ground level inside the tower. The latter has been termed an oubliette, while both are commonly referred to as dungeons, despite the fact that they are constructed of finely dressed ashlar and occupy the entire inner areas of the towers. While they may have been used from time to time for the incarceration of prisoners, I believe such chambers were originally intended for more domestic purposes, such as storerooms for grain. Recent investigation into similar chambers has proved the latter to be common usage, with the temperature maintained at a constant level around 56deg. F.

61. Pevensey Castle: several periods of defence are represented in this view. The fallen walls to the right and left foreground are Roman; the main block is the remains of the Norman keep; the curtain wall beyond is mostly 13th century; while the horizontal slots are ingeniously contrived pill-boxes of the 1939-45 war, so designed as to resemble parts of the original castle.

The earthworks and water-filled moat of the castle survive in very good condition. The only part of the fort to contain substantial earthworks was the southern section, where they survive in relatively good condition, though the walls themselves have long since collapsed at this point. Standing in the castle courtyard is an exceptionally well-preserved cannon. It dates from Elizabeth I's reign and was one of two demi-culverins used to arm the castle in 1587, one year before the Armada. It was made in the Sussex weald and is embossed with Elizabeth's insignia. The carriage is a modern, authentic replica and beautifully made, showing the ingenious method of constructing such carriages for speedy assembly and dismantling.

The castle was presented to the Office of Works (now the Department of the Environment) in 1925 and was still undergoing restoration at the outbreak of war in 1939. In May 1940 it was provisioned with a number of ingeniously contrived pill-boxes, so disguised as to resemble parts of the original fabric. The three drum towers of the inner bailey were also used to garrison soldiers of the British, Canadian and American armies, and also the Home Guard. They received their present brick-lined 'skins' at this time. After the war it was decided to leave most of these additions to the castle as an important phase in the castle's history, for once again Pevensey had been called upon to fulfil its ancient function of defending the 'Invasion Coast'.

Rye

(Ria. Rya. Rye. Island in the sea.)

The picturesque port of Rye began life as an Iron Age hillfort and developed into a town in the early years of the Middle Ages. This stretch of Sussex coast, however, as is shown in the entries for Camber and Winchelsea, then looked very much different than its appearance today. The hill upon which Rye stands and the one opposite, later to be the site of New Winchelsea, protruded well into the sea as rocky peninsulas, protecting between them a natural sheltered haven. Over the centuries violent storms and other factors have changed not only the coastline but also its strategic importance. This vulnerable corner of south-east England is relatively unprotected, and has often come under French influence, both in military and social terms.

Henry II made Rye a member of the Cinque Ports to assist the port of Hastings, which was already declining because its harbour was silting up. The Cinque Ports were an ancient federation first instigated by Edward the Confessor, developed more fully by William the Conqueror, and brought to full effectiveness in the mid–12th century. Their purpose was to protect the south-east coast. In return for special privileges, members of the federation (the original five were Dover, Sandwich, Hythe, Romney and Hastings) had to supply ships and manpower on a rota basis to protect the seas from foreign powers and to forestall any threatened invasion of England.

In 1204 King John lost many of his French possessions, including Normandy, and England was once more on a war footing with France. In 1215 the French Dauphin, Louis, was invited by some of the English barons to overthrow John and take the throne of England, but when John died in 1216 it suited the barons better to send Louis back home in favour of the king's infant successor, Henry III. The French were not to be so easily dismissed, however, and so began a fresh wave of assaults on England's coastal towns.

The title of Constable of Dover castle went along with that of Warden of the Cinque Ports and became acknowledged as a position of distinction. In 1217 Hubert de Burgh held the office and successfully fought a sea battle with the French off Sandwich. In 1249 Henry III ordered Peter of Savoy, then Warden, to build a castle at Rye for the protection of the town and the Channel. Known originally as Baddings Tower, it was erected very quickly but seems not to have had a surrounding curtain wall. Perhaps the sea and its hill-top position were considered protection enough. The tower was about 35ft. square, including the four cylindrical turrets at each corner, had walls 4ft. thick and rose to a height of over 40ft. It survives in almost perfect condition, except for the loss of its parapet.

The tower remained the only stone defence at Rye until the 1330s when Edward III issued successive grants for the building of a town wall, which served as an outer courtyard as in more traditional castles. No sooner were the walls complete than they were put to the test in a series of raids by the French. One especially violent attack in 1339 proved the walls sufficiently weak in places to allow the French to over-run the defences and burn 52 houses to the ground. The walls underwent repair, but the raids still continued, culminating in the devastating attack of 1377 when the entire town was sacked and put to the torch.

63. This view of the Land Gate at Rye shows how little it has changed in the last 200 years— except for the insertion of a clock between the windows above the gateway.

IV. Herstmonceux Castle.

V. Arundel Castle.

A grant by Richard II in 1381 made provision for a new and stronger town wall, to include strong gates guarding the approaches to the town. Fragments of these walls remain today along with the splendid Land Gate, a massive twin-towered structure measuring over 60ft. in width and closely resembling the West Gate at Canterbury, built at about the same time. It was begun around 1340 but was greatly enlarged and strengthened during the 1380s. Houses now huddle up to its walls tending to diminish its great size, but it remains an impressive and formidable structure.

With the strengthening of the town walls, the Ypres Tower (as the earlier castle has later come to be known after one of its 15th-century owners) declined in importance and ceased to be a strategic part of the town's defences. In 1421 it was used as the town hall until a new one was built, the original having been burned to the ground in the 1377 attack. After this time the importance of Rye itself began to decline as the harbour silted up and it was considered safe enough to allow the Ypres Tower to be sold. The purchaser, in 1430, was John de Ypres, from whom it took its new name. It remained in private hands until Rye Corporation, who had rented the building since 1494, purchased it in 1518 for £26. The Corporation converted the tower into a gaol.

The tower gradually fell into disrepair, and demolition was even considered at one time in the early 19th century. Between 1819-21 a brick exercise yard was built against the northern side, which was rebuilt in the 1830s. Four more cells were added between 1837-8 as was the square tower, a little to the east of the tower itself, used to house women prisoners. A hint that slightly 'unbalanced' prisoners were also kept at the Ypres Tower is indicated by the padded walls of the ground floor room of the south-west turret.

Most of those kept at the tower were petty thieves, but occasionally more serious crimes were dealt with. Following the Prison Act of 1865, however, Rye gaol was down-graded to the humble role of lock-up; most of its prisoners were simply town drunks who could not make the journey home after a night of celebration! In 1870 it fulfilled the role of soup kitchen and, after 1891 when it ceased to be used as a gaol, it became a mortuary, thus lowering still further the status of this once proud fortress. The mayor in 1894 complained to the town clerk of the awful stench coming from the mortuary and the filthy conditions within it.

The tower was very nearly let by the council in 1901 as a private house, despite its run-down state. In 1923 it was listed as an ancient monument, put in repair and opened to the public. In 1954 the present excellent museum was established, which function it fulfils today. A

64. This view of the Ypres Tower shows the rectangular tower added in 1837-8 to house women prisoners, during its days as a gaol.

terrace opens out near the top of the tower providing an unrivalled view across Romney Marsh. The attractive little garden, enclosed within brick walls, was formerly the exercise yard and now makes a pleasant picnic spot on a summer's day.

The delightful town of Rye demands attention and careful exploration. Its cobbled streets and ancient houses—particularly the *Mermaid Inn,* pottery and gift shops, and, of course, the splendid Land Gate and Ypres Tower—are reward enough, and as a bonus is the beautiful countryside in which the town stands.

65. The 14th-century Strand Gate, Winchelsea, viewed from the townward side.

Winchelsea

(Winceleseia. WInchenesel. Winchelsay. Winece's stream. N.B.—Applies to 'old' Winchelsea, not the 'new' town of Edward I.)

Although nearby Camber castle has often been referred to as 'Winchelsea Castle' in old documents, Winchelsea proper never had a castle. It was, however, a very important hill-top town completely encircled by a defensive wall (which justifies its inclusion here), for the town was regarded in medieval times as being a fortress in its own right. Some maps indicate a site known as 'Castle Field' near to St Leonard's church, but there is no evidence to suggest that a castle was ever built there. Perhaps the town's walls and hill-top setting were considered adequate defence.

The ancient port of Winchelsea lay on level ground a little further seaward, but the encroachment of the sea and the frequent violent storms in that area in the 13th century threatened its existence. The port, however, was still considered very important, particularly since in the late 12th century Henry II made the town, along with Rye, a member of the Cinque Ports because of the silting up of Hastings harbour. In 1280 Edward I decided to rebuild the town in a safer place, choosing the higher ground to the north on which the present town stands. It is hard to visualise the importance of the site today for the sea once came considerably further inland, and in the 13th century the twin hill-tops of Winchelsea and Rye were peninsulas jutting out into the sea. In February 1288 a particularly violent storm destroyed the old town, which for a short while had co-existed with the new.

The new town was first laid out in October 1283 by Stephen de Penchester, Warden of the Cinque Ports, by order of Edward I. There then followed a remarkable exercise in town planning. The hill-top on which New Winchelsea was built approximated to an isosceles triangle in shape, covering an area of about 150 acres. The land was divided into a neat grid pattern of wide, spacious streets. All the houses were substantially built and arranged around 39 neat rectangular blocks. Although the town never attained its intended status and has since declined, many of the surviving houses are either medieval or contain medieval features, and are in fine condition. A remarkable series of

119

cellars survive beneath many of the houses, designed, it is believed, not only for storage, but also for shelter should the town be attacked.

Two churches, those of St Thomas and St Giles, had stood in the old town, with a monastery of the Grey Friars and three hospitals; all were allotted sites in the new town. Winchelsea was regarded as a model town and would have flourished had the sea, its main source of income and the principal reason for its existence, not deserted it, and thus been responsible for changing the town's fortunes twice in its history. Perhaps, though, it is fortunate for us today that 'progress' has decided to pass by Winchelsea for it is one of the most complete medieval towns in the south. It has a lazy, half-forgotten, but altogether enchanting atmosphere about it, as though caught in a deep and prolonged sleep, waiting to be woken and hurried into the 20th century.

The summit of the hill was enclosed by a defensive wall to encircle the town, and every approach road into the town was protected by a gate. Three of these gates still survive, the Pipewell, Strand, and New Gates, but almost the entire circuit of the town wall has been destroyed.

The Pipewell, or Land Gate, was destroyed by one of many French attacks in 1380 and rebuilt in about 1510. It is a comparatively small structure measuring only about 16ft. by 13ft. internally above the gateway, which was vaulted, with walls 3ft. thick. The New Gate originally protected the southern-most entrance to the town. It, too, is a fairly small structure. Where it met the town wall a passage was formed measuring about 10ft. by 11ft. and was, like the gate-passage, also vaulted. Recesses were formed where the town walls abutted the passage, but have been partially blocked in recent times. The New Gate now stands isolated on the road to Hastings and marks the intended southern limit of the town—a limit that was never reached, for the sea receded faster than the expected wave of prosperity could advance.

The third gate to survive, and easily the most impressive, is the Strand Gate guarding the road to Rye and overlooking the ruins of Camber castle. It dates from the 14th century and was protected to front and rear by two cylindrical towers and a portcullis at either end of the gate-passage, which was vaulted. The left-hand tower of the outer face has a doorway giving access to a small chamber. The other three towers were only accessible from the battlement walk above. There is also a large machicolated-type opening at parapet level running the full length of the east wall of the gate.

Magnificent views are afforded from the Strand Gate, the land falling away dramatically to the marshy levels below. Had the town prospered, Winchelsea would have provided us with an interesting 'cross-breed' of castle and fortified town, for lords and ordinary townsfolk alike lived alongside one another within its walls. As it is, we are left with three ancient relics of its defences brooding over this forgotten landscape and offering us a hint of what might have been.

66.   View of the Strand Gate, Winchelsea, showing the entrance passage and vaulting.

The Lost and Minor Castles

Aldingbourne

Horsfield said of Aldingbourne castle in 1835:

> Formerly in this parish were a park and mansion house, belonging to the See of Chichester, and used by the bishops as an occasional summer residence. The mansion received additions and improvements from successive bishops, till the fanatic zeal of Waller's soldiers, at the siege of Chichester, having plundered the Bishop's Palace, counselled the destruction of this episcopal dwelling. They stopped here on their march to Arundel, and levelled it with the ground.

The castle started life as a simple motte and bailey but soon acquired a small stone keep. The bishops of Chichester gradually converted the site into a comfortable dwelling, and it became one of their favourite residences. Robert de Stratford died there in 1362, and in 1536 Robert Sherborne left £10 towards the cost of building a new tower. By 1606, however, it had so fallen into decay that Bishop Lancelot was instructed to demolish it. The order was apparently ignored, and it remained standing until Waller destroyed it in 1643. It was afterwards sold in 1648, when parts of the main dwelling and chapel were still standing. It is now down to foundation level, the materials being taken at various times for road construction; an all-too-familiar tale with Sussex castles.

The site was excavated by the Sussex Archaeological Society in 1969, who began by stripping away the dense scrub smothering it. It was found to cover an area of about 2¾ acres and fragments of the original mound and earthworks were found, though badly mutilated. The mound was oval in shape with the keep positioned slightly north of centre. Virtually no trace of the curtain wall remains, but about half the foundations of the keep survive. It was built from flint rubble, lined on the outside with knapped flints, and on the inside with courses of Selsey limestone. The keep was comparatively small—only about 39ft. square externally—with walls 9ft. thick at the base, and there was a well in the basement.

Most of the foundations discovered on excavation were infilled with earth to protect them, and today all that remains above ground are some insignificant little bumps in a field. Because few indications of a later period were found, it is now thought possible that this was not the site of the bishop's castle, which may lie elsewhere—though this seems unlikely.

Burghlow

Earthworks alone mark the spot where Burghlow castle once stood, guarding the valley of the river Cuckmere. It was of the motte and bailey type, the mound standing in the northern section, with the ground falling sharply away all around it. A comparison has been drawn in the past between it and Bramber castle, and the two are remarkably similar, even allowing for the lesser stature of Burghlow.

The builder and subsequent owners of the castle are not known, and it seems never to have been a very substantial structure. Apparently there were some stone buildings, for during the excavations last century foundations were uncovered. In those early days of archaeology, however, the excavators removed the stone and used the materials to build two barns in the vicinity. A few bones and scraps of pottery were also found.

Horsfield, writing in the first half of the 19th century, suggested that Henry VIII may have built one of his coastal castles here to protect the Cuckmere, which was then a navigable river. He also mentions a similar castle at Chinting.

Caburn

The site now occupied by Caburn castle has been fortified since the Iron Age. The first fortifications took the form of a hillfort, built in about 150 B.C. on the site of an undefended enclosure of around 500 B.C. These were successively heightened by the Romano-British in about A.D. 300 against Saxon raids, and again in the 12th century.

Excavations carried out by the Sussex Archaeological Society in 1937–38 revealed a 12th-century cooking pot, a row of post-holes on part of the ramparts, and a series of grain storage pits. The castle seems never to have been fortified in stone and nothing is now known of it, except that it was deserted at an early date. It was briefly called into action, however, in 1940 when the Home Guard refortified part of it with trenches.

Earnley

The name Earnley comes from two Saxon words, 'earn' and 'lege', which means 'the abode of the eagles'. Though it is doubtful whether eagles would have been found in the area, the name gives some indication of how wild and inaccessible this part of Sussex once was. Later, during the reign of Edward I, it gave its name to the family of Ernlé, who for a long while were one of the most influential families of West Sussex.

Near the parish church they built their family home. It was never a substantial castle but rather a fortified manor house, once quite extensive and surrounded by a moat. Virtually nothing of the original house remains now. The most influential and distinguished member of the family was Sir John Ernley, who was Chief Justice of the Common Pleas during Henry VIII's reign.

Ewhurst

Ewhurst castle, in Shermanbury, was once a substantial building, though it seems to have been only lightly defended. What remains today of the original castle is the 14th-century gatehouse, though considerably restored, and part of the moat.

Fulking

There appear to have been two castles at Fulking—one a motte and bailey, the other a fortified manor house called Perching castle. The motte and bailey may have been deserted at an early date (for no masonry appears to have been erected on the site), perhaps for another manor nearer the village. It would certainly seem unlikely for both castles to have been in active use at the same time.

On the summit of Edburton Hill and close to Iron Age and Romano-British settlements can be seen the clearly-defined earthworks of a motte and bailey castle, known as Castle Rings. It is very small, consisting of a mound and an attached rectangular bailey, but is relatively undamaged and shows up well on aerial photographs. The site was almost certainly occupied in prehistoric times and later provided an ideal nucleus for a Norman motte and bailey. Its isolated position today on the crest of the South Downs makes it difficult to determine its original value, but a glance at old maps reveals much more. It lies immediately beside the ancient division between the Rapes of Bramber and Lewes, which is also the boundary between East and West Sussex. When the Normans established themselves as controllers of the six rapes, Fulking castle was probably an ideal vantage point overlooking both the Downs and the Weald.

It is unlikely to have been considered important in the later Middle Ages: on the contrary, its exposed position away from any settlement would have been a decided disadvantage, which possibly explains why the site was never fully developed. There are indications in the vicinity of terraces, probably cultivation marks dating from the Iron Age, when the Downs were relatively densely populated. Nearby are the massive Iron Age defence works of the Devil's Dyke hillfort.

To add to the confusion of there being two castles here, Fulking also possessed another manor, owned at the Conquest by Godfrey de Bellomonte. It passed to Robert Aguillon and at his death in 1286 he was also in possession of at least part of the manor of Perching. Both Fulking and Perching manors formed part of Edburton parish and were located in the Hundred of Poyning.

The present manor house at Perching stands about 300 yards west of the village, adjoining a large farmhouse. Neither of these is the site of Perching castle, which lay in a field 300 yards further west of the farmhouse. It is now marked by a large, square mound with traces of a moat just visible. The castle stood in the middle of a large field, the adjacent road and hedges being slightly diverted to avoid

the moat, which is now dry. Nothing remains above ground, though low stone walls were still visible during the 19th century.

Earl Warenne was the overlord of Perching and Fulking manors, which were held from him by a certain Tezelin, said to be Warenne's cook. Perching later came into the possession of the Aguillon and the Percyng families, who took their name from the manor. In 1327 the manor was in the hands of Sir Robert de Arderne, who received a licence to crenellate his manor house two years later. The earthworks of Perching castle remaining today would indicate that it was never a very substantial structure and was probably a fortified manor, similar to Hever, in Kent. The manor passed in 1412 to Robert de Poynings and afterwards to Sir Anthony Browne, but it is not known when the castle was pulled down to make way for the present manor house.

The early history of the manor of Perching is so closely entwined with that of Fulking it seems impossible to disentangle it. A great many landowners also had parcels of land within the parish of Edburton, which further adds to the confusion. Unfortunately, we have neither the space nor the scope to unravel their histories here and must content ourselves with substantiating the existence of two quite separate castles.

Hartfield

This is another motte and bailey castle site, deserted at an early date, which seems never to have had its timber defences replaced in stone. It is freely accessible to the public by means of a footpath (clearly marked 'Castlefield leading to Motte Field'). The motte now stands only about 6ft. high, but its outline is more-or-less complete. Attached to it are the scant remains of the bailey ramparts.

Iden (La Mote)

Iden castle was actually a fortified manor house. The manor of Moat, or La Mote, is first recorded in 1318, though it is doubtless much older. Its owner, Sir Edmund de Passeley, received a licence to crenellate his manor house in that year. After his death in 1339 it was held by his widow, Margaret, who in turn bequeathed it to her sons. It descended successively to each of three sons, Thomas, Edmund and Robert, after whom it passed to the latter's grandson, another Robert.

In 1411 the manor was divided into three parts (a situation no doubt arising from the successive inheritance by each of Sir Edmund de Passeley's three sons). William Swynbourne held one third of it; a second third was held by William Marchant and William Marney; the third part was owned by Robert Passeley's widow. Swynbourne had married this lady, so on her death in 1420 he thus came into possession of controlling shares in the manor. However, in 1453, it is recorded that Robert Passeley's eldest son, Sir John, died in possession of the whole manor.

It then passed to his son, another Sir John who, in 1460, conveyed it to John Scott. It later passed to Sir Nathaniel Powell in about 1656 and was acquired by Mrs. Catherine Owens of Iden Manor in 1769.

Midhurst

A Norman motte and bailey castle once stood on St Anne's Hill at Midhurst, long before the present Cowdray castle was built in the late 15th century. Near to the church, and close by the river Rother, is a roughly triangular-shaped mound with an attached bailey, separated from it by a ditch. Only a few traces of stone walling remain, but excavations in 1913 revealed much of interest about the site.

The enclosure was surrounded by a 15ft.-thick coursed rubble wall which was further sub-divided by a cross-wall to create an inner bailey. Butting against the east curtain wall were a hall and a chapel, while on the mound itself were found traces of a shell keep. All were built in stone, the decoration of which suggests the mid–12th century

VI. Bodiam Castle.

as the time of construction. The site appears to have fallen into disuse at an early date and little is known about it, except that it was once the property of the Bohuns. They are believed to have abandoned the site towards the end of the 13th century in preference for that now occupied by Cowdray castle, a magnificent semi-fortified mansion on the opposite side of the river. When Sir David Owen inherited estates at Cowdray in 1492, he, too, elected to build his new castle on this new site, away from the original castle at Midhurst.

Old Erringham

An interesting, though long deserted, earthwork has the remains of what looks to be a Norman chapel within its precincts. The castle was of the motte and bailey type and seems never to have been re-fortified in stone. A V-shaped ditch and rampart surround the central area, the bank of which was found on excavation to overlay coins dating from the time of Aethelred II (992-8), indicating a Saxon origin for the earthwork. It was strengthened during the 12th century (pottery of that date was found) by a timber palisade. Post-holes, placed about 8ft. apart, were traced around the top of the bank. Never very substantial, the castle seems to have been deserted later in that century, perhaps during the reign of Henry II when many adulterine castles were destroyed.

Pulborough

There was a motte and bailey castle at Pulborough, known as Park Mount, but the site is now much overgrown, making it impossible to visualise it as it once was. It has many similarities with Knepp castle, and consisted of a mound at the northern end encircled by a ditch and rampart. Attached to this and protecting its other three sides was another ditch and rampart enclosing the bailey area. The whole site, but particularly the mound, has been disturbed at some time, probably for its materials. Originally it commanded a position overlooking the river Arun and would have had a good view of the surrounding countryside. It does not appear to have been a castle of importance, and no historical data is available.

Rogate (Haben Bridge)

Apart from the fact that a small castle is known to have existed at Rogate, there is nothing to add to Lower's statement in 1870:

> On an eminence above the Rother are some vestiges of a fortified residence within a fosse, but of its origin nothing seems to be known.

Rudgwick

The Ordnance Survey maps indicate three castle sites around Horsham. Two of these remain lost, while of the third, that of Rudgwick (sometimes called Lynwick), virtually all trace has disappeared. It was built by the de Sauvage (or Savage) family, of nearby Sedgwick castle, but nothing is known of it. The site was excavated in 1923 when slight remains of stone walling were found. It appears to have been circular in plan, similar to Sedgwick, with which it has often been confused.

Sedgwick

The scanty remains of Sedgwick castle are to be found about 2½ miles east of Horsham in a thickly wooded part of the county. They are difficult to locate and stand in Sedgwick Park, a much later and still private estate. For many years Sedgwick was likened to other minor castles in Sussex which served as secondary residences or hunting lodges to the lords of more important castles. For example, Verdley castle was a hunting-tower of Cowdray, Knepp of Bramber, Hartfield of Pevensey, and Stanstead of Arundel. These hunting lodges sometimes took the form of small castles, while at other times they were single, unattached towers. When hunting in the densely forested Sussex countryside—and it should be remembered, the chase was considered an extremely important part of a medieval lord's life—such overnight stops and places of refuge would have been necessary. They were not locked between visits by the baron, but most probably were maintained by a small, perhaps independent, household, who would keep the lodge, or castle, in good order and entertain the lord when he arrived.

The Rev. Edward Turner, writing in 1855, however, cast a new light on Sedgwick castle. He was a meticulous and thorough researcher, but could find no documents proving Sedgwick's appendage to any of the major overlords. Instead, he discovered that the castle was an entirely independent residence, owned for over 200 years by the de Savage family. They were the early lords of Broadwater, in which parish Sedgwick castle stood, and had considerable estates in the Rape of Bramber. The first lord was Robert le Savage, who is recorded in the Domesday Survey as holding lands directly from William de Braose, of Bramber, in addition to Sedgwick.

The next four heirs to the Savage estates were all Roberts. Nothing is known of the first three, but the fourth appears briefly in the Exchequer records when he complained to King John in 1197 about the behaviour of a certain John le Combe. Apparently, le Combe's daughter, Agnes, was betrothed, under feudal privilege, to Savage, but she seems to have been married off to someone else. The outcome is not known but Robert le Savage did marry her eventually, having an only daughter, Hawisa, who married twice, the second time to one of the de Nevills. In a dispute with William de Braose in 1268 concerning the collection of murage (the right of a lord to collect taxes from estates held in appendage for the repair of his castle) the castle passed into de Braose's hands. On Hawisa's death soon afterwards the castle remained partly in de Braose's hands and partly in Robert le Savage's.

In 1272 John le Savage exchanged Sedgwick for other lands within the Honour of Bramber and so, after more than 200 years, the castle passed out of Savage ownership.

A licence to crenellate Sedgwick was granted in 1259, though it is quite likely that the earlier manor already had some defences. Immediately prior to John le Savage's exchange with William de Braose the castle was briefly held by Simon de Montfort, but le Savage repossessed it after the Battle of Evesham. In 1290 de Braose died and Sedgwick remained part of the family estate. It is doubtful if the de Braoses ever lived there, but it may at this time have been used briefly as a hunting-lodge. It passed from them to the Says, Herons, Grevilles, de Mowbrays and later to the Howards, afterwards Dukes of Norfolk.

The later history of Sedgwick is obscure, and it is not known when it ceased to be used as a residence. Although small, it was substantially built of stone, and was not merely a hunting-lodge or fortified manor house, as has been suggested. Until about 1850 considerable portions of the castle survived, including the remains of at least one tower, the entrance gateway and parts of the curtain wall and courtyard buildings. Turner himself witnessed many hundred loads of stone being carted away from the castle in his day, a process which has continued into our own times, so that now only the most meagre fragments of wall remain.

Fortunately an accurate plan of the castle was drawn by Mr. Robert Shepherd in 1855 before too much damage had been done to the site. It reveals the castle to be circular, about 200 yards in circumference, possessing a unique system of double moats. A large sheet of water, enlarged out of the outer moat, is to be seen today while the rest of the site, which was excavated in 1923, is now heavily overgrown.

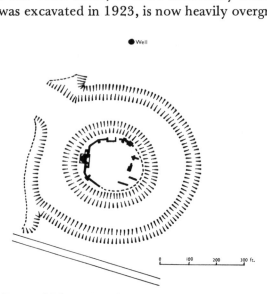

Ground Plan of Sedgwick Castle

Shoreham

Like Horsfield, writing in 1835, I, too, was unable to discover anything about the castle at Shoreham:

> Shoreham appears to have had a castle formerly, but where situated it is now impossible to determine; no remnant standing nor any tradition relative to its site. It, and the manor, was held of the barony of Bramber.

Verdley

Many Sussex castles have been demolished for their materials, particularly for road-making. Bramber and Knepp, among others, owe their present condition to this, but seldom has the destruction been so complete as at Verdley, near Fernhurst, where the castle has been entirely rooted out, including its foundations.

Verdley manor formed part of the Honour of Petworth, in the Rape of Chichester. It is not mentioned in the Domesday Survey but appears to have been the property of the de Bohun family of nearby Midhurst, and later of Cowdray castle. It is supposed to have consisted of a single tower only, measuring some 68ft. by 33ft. with walls 5½ft. thick and surrounded by a dry ditch—the lie of the land would have made a wet moat impossible. In early maps of Sussex it is depicted with a pale-fence enclosing it and, because of its position in Verdley Park, is presumed to have been a hunting-tower, or secondary residence. In the absence of any additions to the tower this would seem to be a fair assessment, but we are unlikely ever to know for sure. With the removal even of the foundations, the site cannot be excavated to provide satisfactory verification.

Two other, rather more colourful, alternatives have been suggested, however, neither of which can be substantiated. The first is that the building was a grange belonging to the monks of Shulbrede. The second claims that the tower was, in fact, a mad-house, attached to the nunnery of Easebourne! More reliable, perhaps, is the assertion that an earlier fortification once stood on the site, which was thrown down by the

Danes. A very sketchy ground plan, dated 1770, survives showing three window openings in the Early English style.

The castle had long been used as a convenient quarry, but in 1880 a large gang of workmen was employed to rout out every single stone—above and below ground—for the construction of rides (or bridleways) through Verdley Wood. Mr. S. E. Winbolt, writing in 1934, visited the site in March that year and reported that 'there is now not a stone left in situ'. A plantation of fir trees has since obliterated the site and its precise location is now known only to a handful of locals.

The slightest remains of banks and ditches can be see today, but it is not known whether these are of original earthworks or the result of the castle's wholesale destruction. The stone rides and paths through the woods can still be seen, but now, alas!, are little used, making the loss of this tower even more poignant.

Camden's description of the castle still holds good—'. . . a lonely and romantic place known only to those that hunt the marten cat'.

— □ —

Castles are also known to have existed at Rotherfield (Castle Hill), Mountfield, Clay Hill, Owls, Dallington Farm, Ford, Barkshale Wood, Halnaker (Boxgrove), and Selham, though virtually all traces have now disappeared. Very little is known of them from written sources, though a few still preserve their earthworks—of which Selham is probably the best example.

The South Downs are covered with ancient hillforts and enclosures of prehistoric date and their earthworks have often been confused with those of castles. Hollingbury and Saxonbury Hills are two such sites frequently referred to as castles. While many prehistoric earthworks form the nucleus of later castles, these two examples seem never to have been so developed. Further discussion of these more obscure earthworks is beyond the scope of this book and must await another opportunity.

Later and Sham Castles

67. Exterior view of the gatehouse
Bolebroke Castle. The rest of it has
been considerably reduced in size.

68. (above) A very rare photograph of Eridge Castle taken just
prior to its destruction in 1938-39.

69. (right) A 19th-century print
of Knepp New Castle, viewed
from the park.

Bolebroke

Bolebroke castle was never intended to be a fortress of the medieval type, but used castellated features as an architectural embellishment. It is doubtful if the house itself could have withstood even the feeblest of assaults, but the gatehouse is substantially built and would have provided at least adequate shelter during times of trouble.

The manor of Bolebroke at one time was the property of the Dalyngrigges, who probably had some kind of residence there, though it is not known whether it was ever fortified. The principal remains today are of the gatehouse, while nearby stands a much altered brick house, first built in the 16th century. Originally it must have been a mansion of some considerable size and what is left is still very impressive.

The gatehouse is roughly square with tall polygonal turrets to the outside. These are covered by bronze ogee caps, but were possibly battlemented in their original form. The inside face was not provided with turrets, having instead large buttress shafts running the full height of the building. The gatehouse is the least altered part of the 'castle' and represents a fine, early example of a brick-built building. It has recently undergone a minor facelift, and when I called the owner was busy removing plant growth from between the bricks and rendering the wallface.

Bolebroke passed, by the marriage of Margaret, daughter and heiress of Sir Edward Dalyngrigge, to the Sackvilles. The Tuftons, Earls of Thanet, next succeeded to it, also by marriage, and they bequeathed it for charitable purposes. It seems to have suffered some neglect at this time and may then have been reduced to its present size.

In 1770 it was sold to Lord George Germain by decree of the Court of Chancery. When he was created a peer he took the title of Baron Bolebroke. He lived there only 20 years, however, and in 1790 it was acquired once again by the Sackvilles when Frederick, 4th Duke of Dorset and Viscount Sackville, purchased the site.

The house today stands close to the busy A264 road, but lies up a narrow and almost inaccessible private track. It is surrounded by large, pleasant gardens and is reminiscent of Sissinghurst castle in Kent —another of the houses acquired by a member of the Sackville family.

Castle Goring

Castle Goring is a paradox among English castles. It polarises the opinions of those who view it, so that one either likes it immensely and is captivated by its unique air, or one despises it. This is caused by its design—from the front almost pure Gothic, classical from the rear, while the interior is a bizarre blend of both styles with a liberal sprinkling of baroque. The designer was either an artist of pure genius or an eccentric suffering from schizophrenia!

The manor of Goring itself has a surprisingly long history, being one of three manors in the district. At Domesday all three were held by William de Braose and formed part of the Rape of Bramber. Later they were consolidated to form one large estate and passed to the Albini family, Earls of Arundel, who subsequently granted it to Roger de Monte Alto. The manor next passed to the de Goring family, who took their name from the estate and later became one of the most influential families in Sussex. Passing through the female line, it next came into the possession of Henry Tregoz of Cornwall, who was much favoured by Henry II. It remained in the possession of his family until the latter part of the 15th century when it passed to Sir John Lewknor. It then briefly became crown property, when Sir John was slain at the Battle of Tewkesbury in 1471.

The manor was afterwards re-acquired by the Lewknors, who managed to hold on to it until the reign of Elizabeth I, when it was purchased by descendants of the Goring family. Sir Bysshe Shelley, the poet's grandfather, purchased it towards the end of the 18th century, and in 1790 he commissioned the architect Biagio Rebecca to design a mansion for him. Whether or not Sir Bysshe was undecided about the style of his new house, the result of this extraordinary partnership is the edifice called 'Castle Goring' which we see today.

The 'castle' stands comparatively unknown on the busy A259 road to Worthing, shielded from view by a thick belt of trees. The entrance front, built from stone and flint, is in pure 'mock Gothick' and consists of three towers equally spaced between lower battlemented wings. The style is a mixture of medieval forms, so that there are, for example, round-headed arches alongside pointed ones, and Norman chevron ornament around Perpendicular windows!

The rear elevation is Graeco-Palladian, as interpreted by Rebecca, and gives no hint of the Gothicisation of the entrance front. The interior is gloriously eccentric and predominantly classical, built around a central dome and spiral staircase, but with the occasional Gothic intervention. The whole effect is exaggerated by the careful choice of materials used. The Gothic sections are mostly built from coarsely dressed stones and flints, but this gives way dramatically to soft white brick and stonework with pink and purple tinges for the classical sections.

Rebecca and Shelley combined their imaginative skills to create this astonishing blend of architectural styles. Much criticised by some, I personally found the place refreshingly light-hearted and altogether enchanting. Today Castle Goring is used as a private school.

Coates

Very little is known about this 'castle' and it has little architectural merit. I mention it here merely because the building has long been known as Coates castle. Horsfield in 1835 wrote:

> A castellated mansion was erected by John King Esq. on an elevated and commanding site. The benefice is united with Bodecton, or Burton, and the church demands no notice.

Dallington Old Castle

The use of the adjective 'old' in its name tends to mislead, since Dallington castle dates only from about 1600 and was added, it seems, purely for romantic reasons. The house stands near the parish church and is built mostly of brick, faced with local sandstone of a very high quality. It consists of a central block with cross-wings and, as far as 'sham castles' go, is a relatively 'quiet' structure.

It has been considerably enlarged over the years, notably in 1910 by Sir E. Newton, and has undergone much reconstruction, though the interior still retains many interesting features; the panelling is of especial note. Newcastle Farm nearby is believed to stand on the site of a small, medieval fortified manor house.

Eridge

Eridge castle can be said to bridge the gap between castles proper and 'sham castles', that is mansions built in castellated style for prestigious reasons with little or no regard for real defensive values. Unfortunately, both the original castle at Eridge and its 'sham' successor have been destroyed, the latter as recently as 1938.

The manor of Eridge once formed part of the barony of Rotherfield and early records would suggest that a substantial house had stood on the site since at least Saxon times. The house was rebuilt in the Middle Ages and, though it is not known to what extent it was fortified, it was considered important enough to warrant a visit by Elizabeth I in 1573. The original castle remained in use to the time of Charles I, and it seems likely that it played some part in the Civil War of that monarch's reign, suffering the usual punishment of being 'slighted'.

In 1787 the manor and lands of Eridge were acquired by Henry, 2nd Earl of Abergavenny, of Kidbrook, near East Grinstead. Employing the services of an amateur architect named Taylor, the earl proceeded to erect for himself a magnificent mansion in the 'Gothick manner'. Parts of the original building were incorporated into the new house, which embodied into its design every conceivable form of Gothic architectural detail. It was, in short, an extravaganza of embattled and machicolated towers and pinnacles, as is revealed through old prints and engravings. In its day it was much criticised for its lack of proportion and feeling for genuine medieval architecture. Murray, in 1877, referred to it as in 'the worst possible taste'.

It was destroyed in 1938-9, which is most regrettable, and replaced by a much humbler residence, itself subsequently reduced in size in recent times. The last two decades have witnessed an upsurge of interest in 18th- and 19th-century Gothic revival architecture, recognising it as an exaggerated imitation of previous art forms, not intended to be a replica of the medieval style, but rather an extension of it. Ironically, had it survived for another 20 years, Eridge castle would today be prized as one of the finest examples of its type.

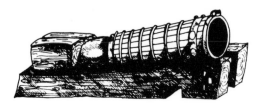

Isfield Place

Isfield Place, once owned by the Shurley family, belongs to a class of semi-fortified buildings of which Ryman's Tower, Appledram; Buckhurst Tower, Withyham; Ratton in Willingdon; Cakeham Tower, West Wittering, and Laughton Place are further examples. They all date mostly from the 15th–16th centuries, though considerably altered in later years, and are built predominantly of brick. They are country mansions, more akin to the later 'sham castles' of the 18th and 19th centuries than to castles proper, and include defences in their designs as a token gesture.

Isfield, probably the most impressive of the group, was described by Lower in 1870:

> . . . formerly very large, and had an enceinte with several towers, more for ornament than defence. A portion of the moat remains, probably belonging to a more ancient structure. The existing building appears to be not older than the time of Elizabeth or James I.

Knepp New Castle

The ancient castle of Knepp, near Shipley, together with its estates, was sold to the Belchers in 1752 and Sir Charles Raymond, Bart., in 1778. It then passed, through his daughter, to Sir William Burrell. Sir Merrik Burrell, Bart., M.P., later acquired the castle and also a large amount of land in the area. When he died he left the Knepp estate to Mrs. Isabella Wyatt and the remainder to Walter Burrell, the second surviving son of his nephew, Sir William. It afterwards passed to Sir Percy Burrell, Bart.

The Burrells built a new and much more fashionable 'castle' about half a mile from the ruins of the ancient castle, screened by trees and extensive parkland, standing in front of an immense 100-acre lake enlarged from a former hammer pond. The castle was begun in 1806 to designs by Nash and is a 'Gothick' castellated mansion of flamboyant proportions. The front elevation is symmetrically arranged around four towers, while the rest of the house is covered with a proliferation of smaller towers and various castellated embellishments. The large circular tower to the rear holds the main staircase.

The interior ground plan of Knepp presents a multitude of odd shapes but they are utilised perfectly to form serviceable rooms. The interior is delightful and sumptuously decorated. It might have been short-lived were it not for the far-sightedness (and obvious wealth) of its owners, for one January night in 1904 the castle burned down. Remarkably, however, the interior apartments were reproduced almost exactly to their original form in the subsequent restoration so that little, if anything, has been lost.

They were not so lucky, though, over the fittings and decorations, which included a marvellous collection of paintings said, by those fortunate enough to have seen it, to be second only to Lord Leconfield's collection at Petworth. Sixteen of the most valuable pictures held there were utterly destroyed, including eight by Holbein and others by Vandyke, Lely and Granger. Some priceless manuscripts and diaries were also lost in the fire. There still remains at Knepp a valuable and interesting collection of paintings, among which are a Rubens portrait of his wife, a head study of Lady Hamilton by Romney, a couple by Jensen, and some of Herring's landscape and animal studies.

One of the former owners of Knepp, Sir William Burrell, Bart., a Kentishman by birth, was a keen historian and archaeologist who was so taken with Sussex that he started a collection of manuscripts and scraps of information with the intention one day of writing an exhaustive history of the county. The famous artists Grimm and Lambert, the latter a Sussex man, were commissioned to illustrate the work, but Sir William's untimely death in 1796 halted the project. The collection, already numbering some forty-odd volumes, was never completed and is now held at the British Library.

Knepp castle is not open to the public and cannot be seen conveniently from the road, but it is nevertheless a most attractive building. It is built, not of stone, but brick covered in stucco and is easily the most impressive of the later and 'sham' castles to survive in Sussex, rivalling even, and perhaps surpassing, the magnificence of the sadly-demolished Eridge castle.

Wadhurst

Wadhurst castle is neither a genuine medieval fortress nor an elaborate 'sham' castle, but a 'modern'-looking house built in 1842. Its only claim to the suffix 'castle' is that its structure contains within it four octagonal towers; otherwise it is an undistinguished and ordinary house.

Genealogical Tables

DUKES OF NORMANDY

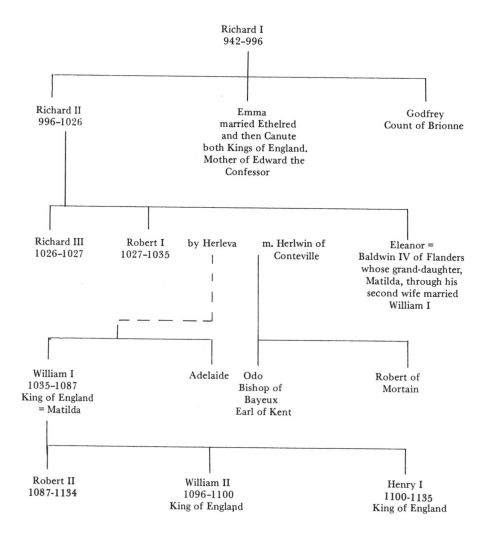

Richard I
942–996

Richard II
996–1026

Emma
married Ethelred
and then Canute
both Kings of England.
Mother of Edward the
Confessor

Godfrey
Count of Brionne

Richard III
1026–1027

Robert I
1027–1035

by Herleva

m. Herlwin of
Conteville

Eleanor =
Baldwin IV of Flanders
whose grand-daughter,
Matilda, through his
second wife married
William I

William I
1035–1087
King of England
= Matilda

Adelaide

Odo
Bishop of
Bayeux
Earl of Kent

Robert of
Mortain

Robert II
1087-1134

William II
1096–1100
King of England

Henry I
1100-1135
King of England

NORMAN AND PLANTAGENET KINGS OF ENGLAND

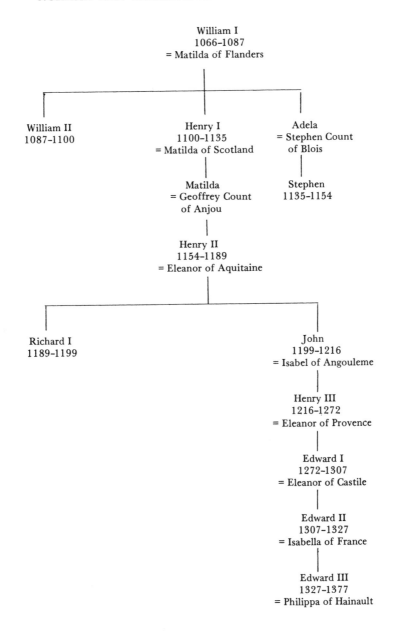

William I
1066–1087
= Matilda of Flanders

William II
1087–1100

Henry I
1100–1135
= Matilda of Scotland

Adela
= Stephen Count
of Blois

Matilda
= Geoffrey Count
of Anjou

Stephen
1135–1154

Henry II
1154–1189
= Eleanor of Aquitaine

Richard I
1189–1199

John
1199–1216
= Isabel of Angouleme

Henry III
1216–1272
= Eleanor of Provence

Edward I
1272–1307
= Eleanor of Castile

Edward II
1307–1327
= Isabella of France

Edward III
1327–1377
= Philippa of Hainault

RELATION OF THE EARLS OF LANCASTER TO THE KINGS OF ENGLAND

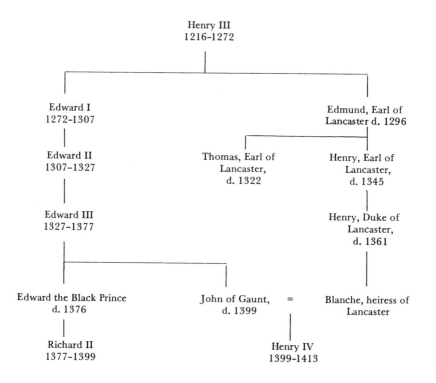

Henry III
1216–1272

Edward I
1272–1307

Edmund, Earl of
Lancaster d. 1296

Edward II
1307–1327

Thomas, Earl of
Lancaster,
d. 1322

Henry, Earl of
Lancaster,
d. 1345

Edward III
1327–1377

Henry, Duke of
Lancaster,
d. 1361

Edward the Black Prince
d. 1376

John of Gaunt,   =
d. 1399

Blanche, heiress of
Lancaster

Richard II
1377–1399

Henry IV
1399–1413

THE HOUSES OF LANCASTER AND YORK

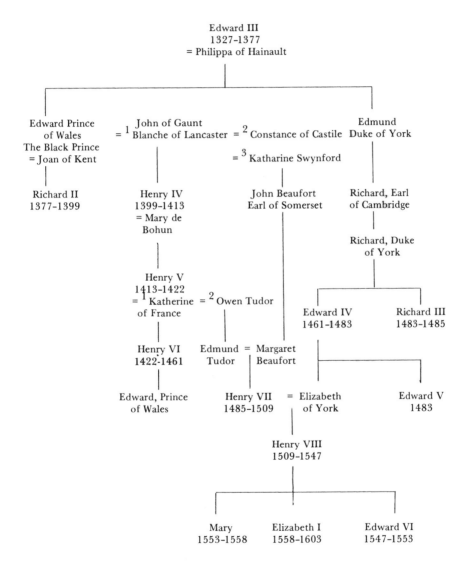

Edward III
1327-1377
= Philippa of Hainault

Edward Prince
of Wales
The Black Prince
= Joan of Kent

John of Gaunt
=¹ Blanche of Lancaster =² Constance of Castile
=³ Katharine Swynford

Edmund
Duke of York

Richard II
1377-1399

Henry IV
1399-1413
= Mary de
Bohun

John Beaufort
Earl of Somerset

Richard, Earl
of Cambridge

Richard, Duke
of York

Henry V
1413-1422
=¹ Katherine =² Owen Tudor
of France

Edward IV
1461-1483

Richard III
1483-1485

Henry VI
1422-1461

Edmund = Margaret
Tudor   Beaufort

Edward, Prince
of Wales

Henry VII
1485-1509

= Elizabeth
of York

Edward V
1483

Henry VIII
1509-1547

Mary
1553-1558

Elizabeth I
1558-1603

Edward VI
1547-1553

THE STUARTS

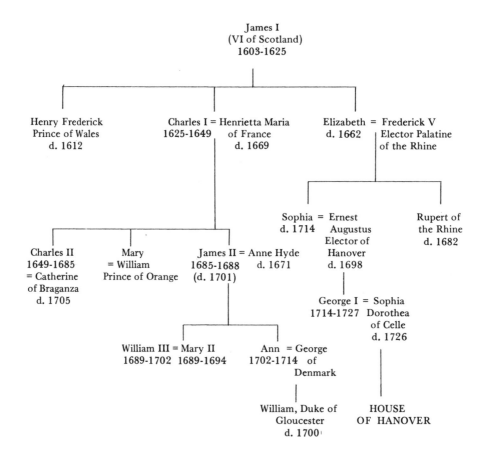

James I
(VI of Scotland)
1603-1625

Henry Frederick
Prince of Wales
d. 1612

Charles I = Henrietta Maria
1625-1649   of France
d. 1669

Elizabeth = Frederick V
d. 1662   Elector Palatine
of the Rhine

Sophia = Ernest
d. 1714   Augustus
Elector of
Hanover
d. 1698

Rupert of
the Rhine
d. 1682

Charles II
1649-1685
= Catherine
of Braganza
d. 1705

Mary
= William
Prince of Orange

James II = Anne Hyde
1685-1688   d. 1671
(d. 1701)

George I = Sophia
1714-1727 Dorothea
of Celle
d. 1726

William III = Mary II
1689-1702 1689-1694

Ann = George
1702-1714 of
Denmark

William, Duke of
Gloucester
d. 1700

HOUSE
OF HANOVER

HOUSE OF HANOVER

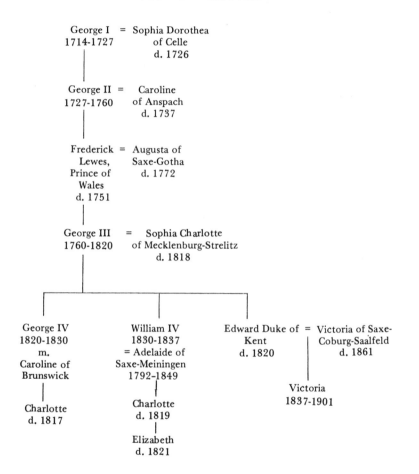

George I = Sophia Dorothea
1714-1727   of Celle
              d. 1726

George II = Caroline
1727-1760   of Anspach
            d. 1737

Frederick = Augusta of
Lewes,   Saxe-Gotha
Prince of   d. 1772
Wales
d. 1751

George III   =   Sophia Charlotte
1760-1820   of Mecklenburg-Strelitz
                       d. 1818

George IV   William IV   Edward Duke of = Victoria of Saxe-
1820-1830   1830-1837   Kent   Coburg-Saalfeld
m.   = Adelaide of   d. 1820   d. 1861
Caroline of   Saxe-Meiningen
Brunswick   1792-1849

                                                       Victoria
Charlotte   Charlotte   1837-1901
d. 1817   d. 1819

                   Elizabeth
                   d. 1821

THE HOUSE OF SAXE–COBURG–GOTHA AND WINDSOR

Victoria   =   Albert of
1837-1901   Saxe-Coburg-Gotha
Prince Consort d. 1861

|

Edward VII
1901-1910

|

George V
1910-1936

|

Edward VIII
Duke of Windsor
1936 (d. 1972)

|

George VI
1936-1952

|

Elizabeth II
1952-

GLOSSARY

Adulterine:	castles built without royal permission.
Allure:	wall-walk on top of curtain wall.
Ashlar:	finely-dressed and squared facing stones.
Bailey:	defended courtyard of a castle.
Ballista:	powerful siege engine discharging heavy bolts.
Barbican:	outer fortified extension to a gate.
Bartizan:	overhanging turret supported on corbels.
Bastion:	projection of wall for additional defence, usually semi-circular or pointed
Blockhouse:	small artillery fort, usually of 16th century, or later.
Buttress:	solid projection from wall face for added strength.
Copings:	protective, often pointed stones on wall top or battlements.
Corbel:	projecting stone from wall face to support floor joists or over-hanging parapet.
Crenel:	notches cut into parapet wall—battlements.
Embrasure:	splayed internal recess of window opening, loop or parapet.
Enceinte:	total enclosure within walls of fortification.
Forebuilding:	entrance tower built against side of keep.
Garderobe:	latrine.
Hoarding:	covered wooden gallery attached to and overhanging wall top.
Keep:	largest and strongest of a castle's towers containing principal apartments.
List:	cleared space surrounding a castle.
Loop:	narrow openings in walls or parapet for observation, to admit light or defence—arrow loops, gun loops.
Machicolation:	overhanging parapet supported on corbels with openings to allow discharge of missiles, etc.
Mangonel:	powerful stone-throwing siege engine.
Merlon:	raised portion of parapet, between crenellations.
Motte:	large earthen mound of early castles, often artificial.
Oilette:	round opening at base of loop, giving key-hole shape.
Oubliette:	dungeon entered from floor of room above.
Portcullis:	iron-covered timber grille, lowered into gate passage in vertical grooves.
Postern:	rear, or emergency gate in castle walls.
Rampart:	originally earthen embankment, later applied to castle walls.
Shell keep:	encircling wall round top of motte, usually with lean-to buildings erected within courtyard space.
Slighting:	deliberate destruction of a castle's defences.
Trebuchet:	powerful siege engine, similar to giant sling.
Ward:	courtyard or bailey.

BIBLIOGRAPHY

Apted, M. R., Gilyard-Beer, R., and Saunders, A. D. (editors), *Ancient Monuments and their Interpretation*, Phillimore, Chichester, 1977.

Armitage, E. S., *Early Norman Castles of the British Isles*, John Murray, London, 1912.

Barlow, Frank, *William I and the Norman Conquest*, Teach Yourself History Series, English Universities Press, London, 1965.

Becket, Arthur (editor), *The Sussex County Magazine*, various volumes, Becket, 1926-34.

Brown, R. A., *English Castles*, B. T. Batsford, London, 1976.

Burke, John, *Life in the Castle in Medieval England*, B. T. Batsford, London, 1978

Camden, William (1551-1623), *Camden's Britannia. Sussex*, published in 1586, Hutchinson, London, 1977.

Churchill, Winston, S., *A History of the English Speaking Peoples*, Cassell and Co., London, 1956.

Clark, G. T., *Medieval Military Architecture*, 3 vols., London, 1884.

Clifton-Taylor, Alec, *The Pattern of English Building*, Faber, London, 1972.

Colvin, H. M. (editor), *The History of the King's Works*, vols. I–III, H.M.S.O., London, 1963-70.

Cook, Olive, *The English Country House*, Thames and Hudson, London, 1974

Cooke, Arthur Stanley, *Off the Beaten Track in Sussex*, Herbert Jenkins (date unknown).

Curzon, Marquis of Kedleston, K.G., *Bodiam Castle, Sussex*, Jonathan Cape, London, 1926.

Davison, Brian K., *The Observers Book of Castles*, Warne, London, 1979.

Fleet, C., *Glimpses of Our Sussex Ancestors*, Farncomb and Co., London (date unknown).

Fleming, Lawrence, and Gore, Alan, *The English Garden*, Michael Joseph, London, 1979.

Forde-Johnson, James, *Great Medieval Castles of Britain*, The Bodley Head, London, 1979.

Garmondsway, G. N., *The Anglo-Saxon Chronicle* (translation), Dent, London, 1953

Gascoigne, Christina and Bamber, *Castles of Britain,* Thames and Hudson, London, 1975

Gies, Joseph and Frances, *Life in a Medieval Castle,* Abelard-Schuman, London, 1975.

Guy, John, *Kent Castles,* Meresborough Books, Rainham, Kent, 1980.

Harvey, Alfred, *The Castles and Walled Towns of England,* Methuen, London, 1911.

Harvey, John, *The Master Builders,* Thames and Hudson, London, 1971.

Horsfield, T. W., *The History, Antiquities and Topography of the County of Sussex,* Baxter, Sussex Press, Lewes, 1835.

Hoskins, W. G., *The Making of the English Landscape,* Hodder and Stoughton, London, 1955.

Howe, W. H. and Evans, Harry, *Castles and Abbeys of Great Britain and Ireland,* vol. I, John Dicks, London, 1902.

Johnson, Paul, *The National Trust Book of British Castles,* Weidenfeld and Nicholas, London, 1978.

Kightly, Charles, and Cheze-Brown, Peter, *Strongholds of the Realm,* Thames and Hudson, London, 1979.

Kinross, John, *Discovering Castles in England and Wales,* Shire Publications, Aylesbury, 1973.

Lower, Mark Antony, *A Compendious History of Sussex, Topographical, Archaeological and Anecdotical,* John Russell Smith, London, 1870.

Lucas, E. V., *Highways and Byways in Sussex,* Macmillan, London (date unknown).

Mawer, A., and Stenton, F. M., *The Place Names of Sussex,* Cambridge University Press, 1929.

Maxwell, Donald, *Unknown Sussex,* The Bodley Head, London, 1923.

Mee, Arthur, *The King's England. Sussex,* Hodder and Stoughton, London, 1936.

Miller, Ray, and Lip, Gerald, *Around Historic Sussex,* Midas Books, 1976.

Mundy, Percy D. (editor), *Memorials of Old Sussex,* George Allen and Sons, London, 1909.

Nairn, Ian, *The Buildings of England. Sussex,* general editor, Pevsner, Nikolaus, Penguin, London, 1965.

Nixon, F. (editor), *Sussex Life Magazine,* various volumes, South Eastern Magazines, Maidstone.

O'Neil, B. H. St J., *Castles,* H.M.S.O., London, 1954.

Page, William (editor), *The Victoria History of the Counties of England. Sussex,* James Street, Haymarket, 1905.

Platt, Colin, *Medieval England,* Routledge and Kegan Paul, London, 1978.

Postan, M. M., *The Medieval Economy and Society*, Weidenfeld and Nicolson, London, 1972.

Quennell, Marjorie and C. H. B., *A History of Everyday Things in England*, vol. I, B. T. Batsford, London, 1918.

Renn, Derek, *Norman Castles in Britain*, John Baker, Humanities Press, 1968.

Smithers, David Waldron, *Castles in Kent*, John Hallewell Publications, Chatham, Kent, 1980.

Smollett, T. A., *A Complete History of England*, printed by James Rivington and James Fletcher, London, 1758.

Spence, Keith, *The Companion Guide to Kent and Sussex*, Collins, London, 1973.

Stenton, Doris Mary, *English Society in the Early Middle Ages*, Penguin, London, 1951.

Sussex Archaeological Collections, various volumes, Sussex Archaeological Society.

Timbs, John and Gunn, Alexander, *Abbeys, Castles and Ancient Halls of England and Wales*, Frederick Warne, London, 2nd edn., 1872.

Toy, Sidney, *The Castles of Great Britain*, Heinemann, London, 1953.

Trevelyan, G. M., *Illustrated English Social History*, vol. I, Longmans, Green and Co., London, 1944.

Tuulse, Armin, *Castles of the Western World*, Thames and Hudson, London, 1958.

Wilkinson, Frederick, *The Castles of England*, George Philip, London, 1973.

Wright, Tom, *The Gardens of Britain. No. 4. Kent, East and West Sussex and Surrey*, B. T. Batsford, London, 1978.

INDEX

Abergavenny, Henry, Earl of, 142
Adeliza of Louvain, Queen, 24, 99
Adulterine castles, 6, 131
Aelfer, 33
Aethelred II, 131
Agincourt, Battle of, 76, 82
Aguillon: family, 129; Robert, 128
Albini: Hugh de, 24; Isabel de, 24;
　Philip de, 53; William de, 24
Alchemy, 100
Aldingbourne Castle, 17, 125-6
Alencon, Earl de, 51
Alfred, King, 22
Alice, Countess of Eu, 69
Alnwick Castle, 99
Amberley Castle, 12-19, 32
Anglo-Saxon Chronicle, 104
Aquila: Gilbert de, 106; Richer de, 106
Arderne, Sir Robert de, 129
Arthur, Prince, 42
Arundel: 18; Earls of, 24, 25, 26, 94,
　96, 140; Castle, 1, 4, 8, 17, 20-9, 42,
　65, 96, 125, 133
Ashburnham, Roger de, 32

Baddings Tower, 114
Bamburgh Castle, 94
Bar, Joan de, 94
Barbicans, 36, 37, 96, 97
Barkshale Wood Castle, 136
Bart, Sir Charles Raymond, 143
Bartizans, 97
Bastions, 8, 46, 47, 48, 51, 104
Battle Abbey, 57
Bayeux Tapestry, 5, 67, 103
Bayham Abbey, 87
Bear baiting, 93
Beaumaris Castle, 6
Becket, Thomas, 69
Belcher: family, 143; William, 88
Belesme, Robert de, 24
Bellomonte, Godfrey de, 128
Bernard, of Savoy, 75
Bevis, 22
Bigod, Hugh le, Earl of Norfolk, 94
Blanche, Princess, 33
Blockhouses, 8, 10, 45
Bloett, Roland, 87
Blois, William de, 93
Bodeham, de, family, 33
Bodiam Castle, 1, 6, 30-9, 65, 82
Bohun: de, family, 55, 131, 135; John
　de, 55
Bolebroke: Baron, 139; Castle, 139

Boleyn, Anne, 26, 99
Bosworth Field, Battle of, 33
Boulogne, Counts of, 93
Brack Mount, 91, 96
Bramber: 85, 128, 134; Castle, 4, 33,
　40-3, 85, 87, 126, 133, 135, 140
Braose: de, family, 85; Matilda de, 42,
　86; Reginald de, 87; William de, 42
　43, 85, 86, 133, 134, 140
Brieuze, 42
Brisco, Sir James, 17
Bristol Castle, 24
British Museum Library, 144
Brittany, Dukes of, 61
Brown, Capability, 101
Browne, Sir Anthony, 56, 57, 58, 129
Bruce, family, 42
Buckhurst Tower, Withyham, 143
Buckler, C. A., 27
Burgh, Hubert de, 113
Burghlow Castle, 126
Burghs, 2
Burrell, Sir William, 143
Burrell-Bart: family, 88; Sir Merrik,
　143; Sir Percy, 143; Sir William, 143,
　144; Walter, 143
Butler: family, 17; John, 17

Caburn Castle, 126-7
Caerlaverock, Siege of, 24, 94
Caernarfon Castle, 6
Cakeham Tower, West Wittering, 143
Camber Castle, 8, 44-9, 113, 119, 120
Cambridge Colleges, 78
Camden, William, 136
Cannons, 8, 45, 107, 111
Canterbury: 16, 115; Castle, 53
Carausius, 104
Caryll, family, 88
Castle Acre Priory, 91, 93
Castle Goring, 9, 140-1
Castle Guard, 2, 6, 31, 61, 76
Castle Hill, 136
Castle Rings, 128
Catherine of Aragon, 45
Cawley, William, 58
Cedwalla, King, 13
Chanctonbury hillfort, 1
Charles I, 43, 100, 142
Charles II, 26, 80, 81
Charles V, Emperor of Germany, 45
Charles, Prince, 58
Chichester: 135; Bishops of, 13, 15, 80,
　125; Castle, 50-3; Cathedral, 13;

Chichester: continued
    Siege of: 53
Chinting Castle, 126
Chowte, Philip, 48
Cinque Ports, 25, 68, 94, 113, 119
Cissbury hillfort, 1
Civil War, 7, 17, 26, 31, 34, 43, 49, 53,
    58, 100, 142
Clare, William de, 61
Clark, G. T., 41
Clay Hill Castle, 136
Cleveland, Duchess of, 80
Cluny, Abbey of, 91
Cnap, de la, family, 88
Coates Castle, 141
Cobham, Sir John de, 32
Combe: Sir John de, 32; John le, 133
Confessor, King Edward the, 33, 67,
    75, 99, 113
Conwy Castle, 6
Cooling Castle, 32
Cornwall: 45; Dukes of, 43, 87
Cornwall, Earls of, 53
Cowdray: Viscount, 58; Castle, 1, 8,
    54-9, 131, 133, 135
Crecy, Battle of, 25
Cromwell, Richard, 58
Crowhurst Castle, 60-3
Curzon, Lord, Marquess of Kedleston,
    31, 32, 34, 37, 38

Dacre: Gregory, 80; Joan, 78; Thomas,
    Lord, 78, 79, 80, 82
Dallington: Newcastle Farm, 136, 141;
    Old Castle, 141
Dalyngrigge: family, 33, 139; John, 33;
    Margaret, 139; Sir Edward, 32, 33,
    62, 139
Deal Castle, 45, 46, 103
Decoration, 8, 16
Defoe, Daniel, 96
Derval Castle, 32
Devereux, Sir John, 62
Devil's Dyke hillfort, 1, 128
Dissolution, 17, 70
Domesday Survey, 33, 75, 133, 135,
    140
Double glazing, 7
Dover: 104, 113; Roman Fort, 103
Drawbridges, 9, 14, 36, 37, 75
Dungeons, 7, 72, 110

Earnley: Elizabeth, 17; Castle, 127
Edburton Hill, 128, 129
Edith, Queen, 99
Edmer, 75
Edward I, 6, 24, 25, 69, 94, 119, 127
Edward II, 24
Edward III, 69, 70, 94, 114
Edward VI, 58
Edwin, Earl, 67

Eleanor, Queen, 94
Elizabeth I, 26, 58, 80, 111, 140, 142,
    143
Ella, 104
Emmet: Baroness, 18; family, 13;
    Thomas, 17, 18
Environment, Department of, 43, 49,
    63, 81, 111
Eridge Castle, 142, 144
Ernle, family, 127
Ernley, Sir John, 127
Etchingham, Sir John, 32
Eu: Counts of, 61, 68, 69, 70, 75;
    Hugh de, 33; Robert Count of, 68
Eustace, 106
Evesham, Battle of, 94, 134
Ewhurst Castle, 127

Fagge, Colonel, 58
Fairlight, 47
Feudal system, 2, 3, 6, 7, 31, 45, 93
Fiennes: John de, 76; Richard de, 78;
    Sir Roger de, 76, 78, 82; Thomas,
    79; William de, 76
Fitzalan: Edmund, 24; family, 24, 25,
    26; John, 24; Mary, 24, 26; Richard,
    24, 25, 94, 95; Thomas, 25; William,
    25
Fitzbald, Robert, 99
FitzHerbert, Matthew, 52
Fitzlambert, Walter, 61
Fitzroy: Henry, 26; Lady Anne, 80
Fitzwilliam, Sir William, 56
Ford Castle, 136
Francis I, King of France, 45
Fremantle, 87
Fretton, William, 15
Friend, Thomas, 96
Frowdys, John, 79
Fulford, Battle of, 67
Fulking Castle, 4, 65, 128-9
Fyrd, 67

Gaols, 52, 115
Garter, Knights of the, 25, 42
Gaunt, John of, 107
Geoffrey, of Anjou, 93
Germain, Lord George, 139
Gilbert, Earl of Gloucester, 94
Godfrey, Walter, 81
Godwin, Harold (Earl, afterwards
    King), 61, 67, 99
Goring: family, 17, 40; John, 17; Sir
    William, 17
Granger, 144
Grantmaisnil, Hugh de, 68
Granville, Henry, 27
Greville, family, 134
Grimm, 144
Grose, Francis, 42
Guldeford, Sir Richard, 45

Gundrada, 91, 92
Gunpowder Plot, 100
Guns, 6, 9, 36, 46, 47, 48, 49, 56, 103

Haben Bridge Castle, Rogate, 132
Hadfield, M. E., 27
Haesten, 68
Halnaker Castle, 136
Hamilton, Lady, 144
Hampton Court, 56
Hardrada, King of Norway, 67
Hare, Dr. Francis, Bishop of
    Chichester, 80
Hare, Rev. Robert, 80
Hartfield Castle, 129, 133
Harwood family, 17
Haschenperg, Stephen von, 45
Hastings: 31, 47, 113, 119, 120;
    Battle of, 21, 61, 103; Castle, 5,
    64-73, 76
Hawisa, 133
Henry I, 24, 92, 93, 99, 106
Henry II, 6, 24, 69, 93, 106, 113, 119,
    131, 140
Henry III, 61, 69, 87, 94, 106, 113
Henry IV, 25, 33, 107
Henry V, 76
Henry VI, 76
Henry VIII, 8, 26, 45, 46, 49, 56, 58,
    69, 70, 99, 126, 127
Henry, Duke of Lancaster, 107
Heron, family, 134
Herstmonceux Castle, 1, 8, 65, 74-83
Hever Castle, 129
Hillforts, 1, 2, 113, 126, 128, 136
Hitler, 103
Holbein, 144
Holland, John, 25
Hollar, 43
Hollingbury hillfort, 1, 136
Home Guard, 111, 127
Hoo, Sir Thomas, 62
Horsfield, T. W., 125, 126, 135, 141
Horsham, 132, 133
Howard: Charles, 27; family, 24, 26,
    27, 42, 134; Katherine, 26; Mary,
    26; Thomas, 26
Hundred Years' War, 31, 76
Hunting lodges, 42, 85, 87, 133, 134
Hythe, 113

Iden Castle, La Mote, 130
Invasion Coast, 103, 111
Isaac Newton Telescope, 82
Isabella, Queen, 87
Isfield Place, 143

James I, 143
James I of Scotland, 107
John, Earl of Richmond, 61
John, King, 42, 43, 51, 53, 69, 86, 87,
    93, 94, 106, 113, 133

Keeps, 21, 22, 24, 28, 29, 34, 41, 51,
    65, 69, 85, 96, 97, 106, 108, 110,
    125
Kemp, Thomas Read, 80, 96
Kent Ditch, 32
Kent, Earl of, 24
Kitchens, 14, 41, 47, 55, 57
Knepp: Castle, 4, 42, 43, 84-9, 131,
    133, 135; New Castle, 9, 88, 143-
    144
Knott, John, 53

Laguerre, 101
Lambert, 144
La Mote, Iden Castle, 130
Lancelot, Bishop, 125
Land Gate, Rye, 115, 116
Latham, Sir Paul, 80, 82
Laufenburg, Rapids of, 57
Laughton Place, 143
Lawson, Reginald Lawrence, 80
Leconfield, Lord, 101, 144
Leeds Castle, 107
Lely, 144
Lewes: Battle of, 94, 106; Castle, 65,
    80, 90-7, 128; Priory, 91, 92, 93,
    94
Lewis, Duke of Bavaria, 33
Lewknor: family, 17, 33, 140; Robert,
    17; Sir John, 140; Sir Thomas, 17,
    33
Licence to crenellate, 6, 13, 16, 32, 56,
    76, 99, 129, 134
Lincoln, Battle of, 93
Lollards, 13
London, 104
Loops, 9, 108
Louis, Prince of France, 53, 87, 106,
    113
Louvain, Joscelyn de, 99
Lower, M. A. 132, 143
Lowther, Colonel Claude, 80
Luffa, Bishop, 13
Lympne, Roman Fort, 103
Lynwick Castle, 132

Machicolations, 14, 34, 36, 75, 76, 97,
    120
Magna Carta, 94
Mantell, John, 79
Marchant, William, 130
Marney, William, 130
Marshall: Gilbert, 106; William, 52, 94
Martello Towers, 46
Mary, Queen of Scots, 26
Matilda, Queen, 24, 93
Maximian, 104
Mercenaries, 6, 31
Mermaid Inn, Rye, 116
Meutrierres, 36
Midhurst Castle, 55, 130-1, 135

Moats, 3, 9, 14, 31, 34, 47, 48, 55, 75, 82, 85, 111, 127, 128, 129, 134, 135, 143
Monceux: de, family, 75, 76; John de, 75, 76; Waleron de, 75; William de, 75, 76
Montague: family, 58; Viscount, 57; Monte Alto, Roger de 140
Montfort: Simon de, 75, 94, 108, 134; Simon de, the Younger, 106
Montgomery: Earl Roger de, 21, 22, 24, 51, 99; Hugh de, 24
Morcar, Earl, 67
Mortain: Counts of, 93, 106; Robert of, 105, 106, 108; William of, 106
Motte and baileys, 3, 4, 5, 22, 41, 51, 65, 68, 69, 85, 91, 125, 126, 128, 129, 130, 131
Mountfield Castle, 136
Mowbray: de, family, 42, 43, 88, 134; Thomas de, 42; Richard de, 52
Murage, 133

Nash, 143
National Trust, 34, 43, 101
Naylor: George, 80; Lady Grace, 82
Nevill, de, family, 133
Newcastle, Duke of, 100
New Gate, Winchelsea, 120
Norfolk, Dukes of, 17, 24, 25, 26, 27, 42
Norman Conquest, 6, 91, 105
Normandy, 103, 113
Northumberland, Earls of, 99
Noviomagus, 51
Nye, family, 88

Odo, Bishop of Bayeux, 68, 106
Offa, King, 61
Old Erringham Castle, 131
Osbert, Osberner, 33
Oswald, Bishop of Selsey, 61
Oubliettes, 110
Owen, Sir David, 55, 56, 131
Owls Castle, 136
Oxenbridge, Thomas, 79
Oxford Colleges, 78

Papillon, family, 42
Paris, Mathew, 42
Parker, family, 17
Park Mount, 131
Passeley: Margaret de, 130; Robert de, 130; Sir Edmund de, 130; Sir John, 130
Peachey, Sir James, 17
Pearson, Sir Weetman Dickinson, 58
Pelham: Lady Joan, 107; Sir John, 62, 76, 107; Sir Nicholas, 79, 80; Sir Thomas, 79
Pellegrini, 56

Pembroke, Earls of, 52, 94, 106
Penchester, Stephen de, 119
Penshurst Place, 28
Peota, 99
Perching Castle, 128, 129
Percy: Algernon, 100; Elizabeth, 100; family, Earls of Northumberland, 99, 101; Henry Lord, 99, 100; Joscelyn, 100; Lady Agnes de, 99; William de, 70, 99
Percyng, family, 129
Peter, of Savoy, 69, 94, 106, 114
Petworth House, 98-101, 135, 144
Pevensey Castle, 65, 67, 68, 75, 91, 93, 102-11, 133
Philip, Prince, 58
Philippe, Queen, 76
Pipewell Gate, Winchelsea, 120
Plantagenet, Hameline, 93
Portcullis, 14, 36, 120
Portsmouth, 104
Powell, Sir Nathaniel, 34, 130
Poyning, Hundred of, 128
Poynings, Robert de, 129
Poyntz, family, 57, 58
Prince Regent, 27, 101
Prussia, King of, 101
Pulborough Castle, 131-2

Ralph, Earl of Westmorland, 62
Rapes, 21, 42, 51, 62, 68, 69, 75, 85, 86, 91, 105, 106, 128, 133, 135, 140
Ratton, 143
Rebecca, Biagio, 140, 141
Reculver, Roman Fort, 103
Rede: Bishop Robert, 14, 15; Bishop William, 13, 14
Reigate, 94
Richard I, 51, 61
Richard II, 25, 32, 107, 115
Richard III, 33
Richard, Earl of Gloucester, 61
Richborough, Roman Fort, 103
Richmond: Dukes of, 26, 53; Earls of, 61, 69, 106
Rivallis, Peter de, 106
Robert, Duke of Normandy, 106
Rochester Castle, 94
Rogate Castle, Haben Bridge, 132
Roger, Earl of Hereford, 91
Roman Forts, 2, 10, 68, 103, 104, 105, 107, 108, 111
Romney: 113; Marsh, 49, 116
Rotherfield Castle, 136
Rotten boroughs, 43
Royal Commissioners, 33
Royal Greenwich Observatory, 81, 82
Roydon, George, 79
Rubens, 144
Rudgwick Castle, 132

Rufus, John, 69
Russia, Tzar of, 101
Rye, 31, 45, 48, 49, 112-16, 119, 120
Ryman's Tower, Appledram, 143

Sackville: family, 139; Thomas, 33
Sandgate Castle, 45, 47
Sandown Castle, 45
Sandwich, 113
Savage: le, family, 132, 133, 134; John
    le, 134; Robert le, 133, 134
Saxonbury Hill, 136
Saxon Shore, 103
Says, family, 134
Scotney: Peter de, 61; Walter de, 61;
    Castle, 32
Scott: John, 130; Sir Walter, 7, 9
Sedgwick Castle, 132, 133-4
Selham Castle, 136
Selsey: 13; Bishops of, 61
Seymour: Charles, Duke of Somerset,
    100, 101; family, 42, 88, 101
Shelley: family, 17; Sir Bysshe, 140,
    141; Sir William, 17
Shell keeps, 28, 69, 91, 96, 130
Sheppey, Isle of, 56
Sherbourne: Bishop, 16; Robert, 125
Shoreham Castle, 135
Shrewsbury Abbey, 21
Shurland Hall, 56
Shurley, family, 143
Sieges, 7, 8, 17, 24, 26, 51, 52, 55, 61,
    75, 94, 106, 107, 108, 125
Sissinghurst Castle, 139
Slighting, 34, 58, 69, 142
Smuggling, 49
Southampton, Earl of, 56
Spanish Armada, 58, 111
Stamford Bridge, Battle of, 67
St Anne's Hill, 55, 130
Stanstead, 133
Stephen, King, 6, 24, 93, 106
St John Hope, Sir William, 58
Strand Gate, Winchelsea, 120, 121
Stratford, Robert de, 125
Strathearne, Earl of, 94
Sudbury, Archbishop, 13
Surrey, Earls of, 25, 33, 70, 92, 93
Surrey, Sheriff of, 78, 94
Sussex Archaeological Society, 96, 97,
    125, 127
Sussex, Earls of, 94

Sussex, Sheriff of, 52, 78, 87
Swynbourne, William, 130

Tenchebrai, Siege of, 92
Tewkesbury, Battle of, 140
Tezelin, 129
Thanet, Earls of, 33, 34, 139
Thynne, Thomas, 100
Tilbury, 58
Tilliol, Humphrey de, 68
Tostig, 67
Tower of London, 7, 33, 100
Town walls, 2, 51, 52, 108, 114, 115,
    119, 120, 121
Tregoz, Henry, 140
Tufton, John, 33
Turner, 101
Turner, Rev. Edward, 133, 134

Underground passages, 18, 43

Vandyke, 144
Verdley Castle, 85, 133, 135-6
Victoria, Queen, 27
Villandraut Castle, 32

Wadhurst Castle, 144
Waller, General Sir William, 17, 26, 34,
    43, 58, 125
Walmer Castle, 45, 46
Wardeux: Elizabeth, 33; family, 33
Warenne: family, 25, 129; John de, 94,
    97; Rainald de, 93; William de, 91,
    92, 93, 94, 106
Warkworth Castle, 99
White Ship, 24
Wilfred, Saint, 13
William I, Duke of Normandy, 3, 21,
    61, 67, 68, 91, 92, 103, 105, 106,
    113
William II (Rufus), 69, 92, 106
William, Lord Hastings, 62, 70
Winchelsea, 31, 48, 49, 113, 118-21
Windsor Castle, 22, 42, 86
Wyatt, Isabella, 143
Wyndham, family, Earls of Egremont,
    101

Ypres, John de, 115
Ypres Tower, Rye, 114, 115, 116
Ysenden: Ralph de, 69; William de, 69

Castles in Sussex

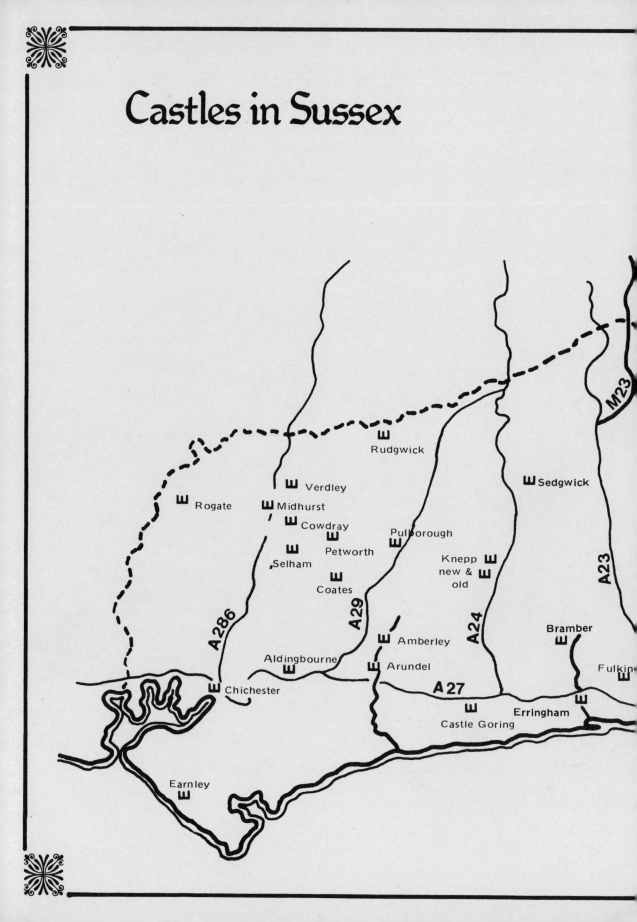